# TALES OF THE KLAMATH RIVER

## A Memoir

ANNE WILSON SCHAEF

# TALES OF THE KLAMATH RIVER
## A MEMOIR

*iUniverse books may be ordered through booksellers or by contacting:*

*iUniverse*
*1663 Liberty Drive*
*Bloomington, IN 47403*
*www.iuniverse.com*
*1-800-Authors (1-800-288-4677)*

*Because of the dynamic nature of the Internet, any web addresses or links contained in this book may have changed since publication and may no longer be valid. The views expressed in this work are solely those of the author and do not necessarily reflect the views of the publisher, and the publisher hereby disclaims any responsibility for them.*

*Any people depicted in stock imagery provided by Getty Images are models, and such images are being used for illustrative purposes only. Certain stock imagery © Getty Images.*

*ISBN: 978-1-5320-5054-1 (sc)*
*ISBN: 978-1-5320-5055-8 (e)*

*Library of Congress Control Number: 2018908213*

*Print information available on the last page.*

*iUniverse rev. date: 11/07/2018*

# CONTENTS

# PROLOGUE

*The great thing about getting older is that you don't lose all the other ages you have been.*
Madeline L'Engle

*I don't have an "inner child." I have the living child who is a full participant and contributor to who I am and who I will become.*
Anne Wilson Schaef

*No journey begins, exists, or ends in isolation. It starts in an ongoing context of processes, is, itself, a process and it only ends when we let it or refuse to remember that all is in context and in process.*
Anne Wilson Schaef

As I read through this manuscript for the final editing, I am aware of how alive, after seventy-eight years, these people, their world and my experiences with them and with my family continue to be for me.

The world in which we were living in these stories is still a world that exists for all of us, yet it is getting buried deeper and deeper as time goes on. Our family, seventy-eight years ago, went from Indian Country in Oklahoma to Indian Country in California – an Indian Country that few white people knew and much of California knew nothing about at that time. The year was 1939, post First World War and pre Second World War. It was a time of interlude, when many still lived in the "old ways."

As I reread what I had written, I realized that there are really three authors to this book.

Of course I give myself, Anne Wilson Schaef, an eighty-three-year-old woman, top responsibility because I actually put the words down on paper.

Then, there is my father, Virgil Eustace Willey, who was gracious enough to record his memories and perceptions before he died. It was very important to him that this story be told and I carried that mandate around with me until, while doing an Ayurvedic cure in India, I found the time to retreat from my busy Western world and "remember." What a joy it was to have the time to relive this precious sojourn with its long-past experiences.

Then, as I read, I discovered a third person had crept into the manuscript as an author too. That five-year-old girl had been patiently waiting for me to "be responsible." She spoke in her own idiom, expressions and perceptions out of her own clarity of memory, which was often much more intuitive, perceptive, visual and different from mine. I was amazed at how clear her memories and her voice were. Often, she had to step forward and say, "No, Anne, that's not quite right. This is the way it was." Invariably, I knew she was right.

Thus, the major author is the five-year-old Elizabeth Anne Willey, who turned out to be the main narrator for this book. That sojourn among the Native people and a broad conglomeration of others was, indeed, a most important time. Many are the times this eighty-three-year-old has gone back to visit that period of my life to integrate and reintegrate the base it formed and solidified for myself and my family's link to our Indian upbringing.

As I reread the manuscript, I was astonished with how often that five-year-old just "took over" with very clear memories. Clearly, she still exists with her very strong identity within me.

I still have that "safe point" inside that she discovered for me and remembering the "real people" and their ways has greater and greater meaning for me.

# INTRODUCTION

## The Beginning of the Journey to Return

I am eighty-three now, yet my memories of those days on the Klamath River are as vivid and real to me as the accumulating age spots on my hands or the creeping pain in my knees as I climb the stairs. I recently drove down from the Canadian line to Los Angeles on Interstate 5 in my son's khaki-green Range Rover. What a glorious trip! I am so intimately familiar with the entire expanse of this great, variedly beautiful and truly magnificent land that driving trips anywhere almost always result in a flood of pungent memories gathered over a lifetime of exploring the obvious and the hidden ways of this country and its peoples. As I said, for some time now, I had been toying with writing a book about our adventures on the Klamath River which began when I was just a month past my fifth birthday and this recent long "road trip" across the country solidified the need to actively start writing. This is a true story of a family, who in 1939, ventured from its safe nest in "Indian Country" in Oklahoma to "Indian Country" in Northern California to gold mine and back again. It is told through the eyes of a five-year-old girl and her father as they lived it with perceptions added by her eighty-three-year-old adult who also lived it. Life and times like these no longer exist!

At that time in our lives, we lived in "Indian Country." In 1939, the area on the border between Northeast Oklahoma and Northwest Arkansas still had a wildness about it that savored its Oklahoma Territory days.

It was, after all, the land where the Cherokee Trail of Tears dropped many of its tattered and shaken traffic of human survivors. It was the land where the five civilized tribes were dumped. It was the land where Zeke Proctor, one of my ancestors, who was the only individual person with whom the federal government ever signed a treaty, prowled in the service of his culture and his people. Jessie James and Belle Starr had sought their kind of justice against the encroaching railroads and corporations for the common people in this part of a world being trampled by industrialization and big business. In the world of my childhood, these "outlaws" were still heroes. I remember how my family bragged that we had an uncle, a banker, who had been shot by Jesse James. Their response always – "Damn fool to draw a gun on Jesse!"

My small world in Oklahoma was inhabited by a people who were quite willing to accept Christianity and go to church – actually, church was fun. And, underneath the Western clothes and Western ways of the white nation, almost underground if you will, was another whole world. This was the world of the Cherokee, the Muskogee, the Chickasaw and the Cree. Everyone was Indian! We just didn't talk about it. It was "assumed." We had to cope with the dominant culture. We didn't have to "live" it or agree with it. Even our form of Christianity, I later learned after we left, had been assimilated into the basic "knowings" of our Indian people.

For us, the rules were:

1) Honor the Creator.
2) Honor all Creation.
3) Be of Service.
4) Preserve the culture, even if underground.

We all lived by these four tenets even when they were unspoken. Honor, respect, honesty and humility were integrated in our life and everyone was "family," whether they knew it or not. We were one with all creation. That's just the way it was and my five-year-old assumed that it was the way the world was – and it was for us – then.

In this underground, more basic world, if you will, the "old ways" were very much alive and well. Everyone I knew hunted and gathered from the abundance of the natural world around us. Everyone came to my great-grandmother for healing. Everyone accepted without mentioning or question that all people were one with one another and with all creation and that we were here to honor the Creator, honor all creation and to serve. It never occurred to anyone around me to ignore that we all were spiritual beings, living in a spiritual world created by the Creator for us all and everyday was an opportunity to give thanks and be grateful for everything we had. Everyone knew that honesty was good and that people who were dishonest could not be trusted – no matter who they were. Humility and spirituality were never spoken of – in fact, we had no words – they were lived. The unseen and unknown were our constant companions.

There was an underlying assumption shared by almost everyone around me that to live in community, harmony, and balance was the natural order of the world. Oh, of course, some people forgot that natural order sometimes or were "misguided." Yet, there was always an assumption that they knew how to behave and had either forgotten or were "not brought up in a good way." There were no "takers" in our small community in Oklahoma. Everyone tried to see that we all got what we needed and strived to give or give back what they could to maintain the natural balance. Maintaining the natural balance was of utmost importance – even my five-year-old knew that.

It was from this "warm bath" of a world that my father, mother and I decided that we would take an indefinite leave of absence from his work, sell all we had, and try our hand at gold mining on the Klamath River in California, which was somewhere way beyond anything we knew or had visited. I say "we" because that's the way things were done in my family. Even though I was very young, I was always in on the discussions and the decision to undertake this adventure was clearly a family decision. My memories of our trip and our time on the Klamath reach deep into my psyche and strongly impacted who I became and who I am today. My desire to write about a time long gone and heroic people who shaped a time and a place had long since been percolating within my being. I had even gone so far as to have my father dictate his memories of the trip before he died over thirty years ago. I had feared that I had lost the tape in moving until I had discovered that I had the transcription of those tapes on paper. But, wait, I'm getting ahead of myself.

First, the present. On this recent trip down Interstate 5, I could feel the excitement building as we left Grants Pass and pushed south into California. We had spent the night in Grants Pass after deciding that we would rather stop to see a movie we wanted to see, *Life as a House,* in some town, any town we were passing through rather than try to push on farther that evening. As it turned out, there had been a heavy snow that night on the pass and we had made the right decision. We were cozy and warm with a fire in the fireplace of the spacious rooms of an off-season, cut-rate executive suite in a grand motel while the December storm spun and raged around us. When we checked out that morning, we were told that chains had been required on the pass the night before and that morning and we should be cautious.

"Not with my son's Range Rover," I commented. "It's all-wheel drive all the time." I felt somewhat smug in his choice of a vehicle and very grateful that he had lent it to us for this winter trip. We had driven from Big Bear Lake, California. As we acquainted ourselves with the Range Rover, we carefully maneuvered it around the icy horseshoe turns of the back way down the mountain, emerging relieved as we transitioned from high mountains to the desert in only 20 minutes, driving through nature's daily light show of afternoon shadows, deep-purple and muted, peaceful reds moving over the undulating desert sandstone. Then, at Victorville, we caught the interstate, which would take us all the way to Montana. After we went through a crowded and irritating Las Vegas, we entered the peace of the "scenic drive" country, crossed a corner of Arizona and then moved up the magnificent width of Utah into Montana, paralleling the mountains on our right almost all the way. I never cease to marvel at the breathtaking beauty, the changing land and the splendors of every dance of light and shadows as the earth offers up its secret beauty specific to each hour of the day or the moonlit night. The drive of fifteen hours is never too long, for the land soothes and entertains the whole time if we remember to allow it to do so. The earth massages the eyes, relieving tense muscles in neck and shoulders. The sounds and smells of the land return the ears, nose and skin to the stress-less vortex of their existence, taking nothing, giving all.

After meetings in Montana, we headed west on Interstate 90. The Clark Fork River was our guide and companion through a breathless land that defies human description demanding that it be taken on its own terms or ignored completely. To try to describe it is an arrogance only the foolhardy or unaware would attempt. I never doze or leave a state of mindful presence while going through it, fearful that some natural awareness might go unnoticed and not be recorded in the secret beauty of my memory. The lushness of orange-pocked, pewter lichen challenges the black-green of the pines and the firs for a definition of green. Mottled, verdant valleys and mammoth, precipitous passes ricochet and reverberate in my brain. Then Coeur d'Alene – a gigantic oasis of water holding the lifeblood of a land in sacred safety, through Spokane and on to the desert-like wheat lands – flat, dry and seemingly uninteresting unless you open more than your eyes. How powerful the starkness, punctuated by lava outcroppings scattered here and there as if dropped by a celestial shaker not unlike the "comma shaker" my college freshman roommate used on her term papers. Yet, these are massive "punctuations" dropped on a land to give definition to its seeming plainness. I drove through this land after Mount St. Helens had blown her top. It was a dreamscape of white mystery. Volcanic ash covered everything. The familiar land of golden wheat fields, patches of irrigated, deep-green alfalfa, and black lava rock were all smothered in a thick, whitish gravy of gray ash. Even the houses, barns and farm implements had been turned into ghosts. The cows were no longer Hereford, Angus or Jersey. They were apparitions of partially deflated parachutes suspended above the gray-white ground with entwined strings for legs that hung down, not seeming to touch reality. Only attenuated movements defined them from their dreamscapes. Little furrows of volcanic ash gave definition to the sides of the road which flowed due west, a black snake separated from and exposed by its ash-white surroundings.

This present trip was not like it had been after Mount St. Helens exploded. My flat land of subtle tones, golden wheat stubble, charcoal earth and slate-colored, life-giving waters was as I remembered it. It had returned to itself. Just when I began to tire of the flatness, and the subtlety of the dried colors of the winter-sleeping terrain, the road plunged precipitously down to the Columbia River. Eons of silent persistent flowing water have carved a gorge so deep and wide that seeing it is always a welcome reminder of the patience of water and that the water and the rocks have been here long before we arrived and will remain long after our passing. As my old ones have said to me, "The rocks and the water have much to teach us if we can learn silently and expectantly to listen with all our being." There is a comfort with that knowing coupled with an inescapable uneasiness as we plunge into and crawl out of the gorge along with other cars, trucks and campers who will occupy this place in space no longer than we will and probably never again with us. There is always something unsettling about being reminded about just how finite we are and how eternal the rocks of the gorge remain, unrelated to, yet one with us.

On to Ellensburg, a surprising oasis that opens us to the promise of the green just beyond and the quiet power of Snoqualmie Pass. What a relieving pass – gradual on both sides, wide roads, no precipitous drops – and beauty, just beauty (except, perhaps, for the clear-cut areas and even they have the hastening beauty of coming back. Oh the promise of regeneration!) With the accompaniment of the crashing, falling, rushing rivers, we cross over into the lushness of Western Washington.

On this trip, we have come to join in ceremonies with the Cherokees who have been displaced from their homeland to the westernmost part of our country. They have banded together to participate in the ceremonies, practice the language, guard and pass on the wisdom, and preserve the Cherokee culture. Our being there is supportive to them and supportive to us as we link back with our ancient ancestors and the wisdom which has always been carefully preserved and protected, though remaining hidden until the prophesized time to share it with a world in desperate longing for its truth.

Then to Orcas Island, that gem of perfection nestled in the Puget Sound as part of the San Juan Islands, home to a living Northwest Indian heritage and named after the elusive and often misunderstood Orca whales. Orcas is a lush, healing haven for all who come there and we always want to linger longer. After a painfully too short stay, we leave Orcas on the ferry, making our way through pale winter flat fields that soon would be covered with rioting splashes of shameless color, as spring ushers in and empties in waves of tulips, evolving into the fullness of berries. Passing these lush, flat fields, we come to the static four-lane rope of Interstate 5 that will pull us all the way to Los Angeles.

So, when we reached Grants Pass on this particular trip and we rose not too early as is our style – rolling out about nine and getting on the road about ten (we always say we will get an "early start" and have discovered 10 a.m. is an early start for us), all seemed as it should be. The storm had passed and sunlight ricocheted off the fresh snow, bounced into our rested eyes and faces, and welcomed the new day. Leaving late has its advantages. The road was plowed and mostly clear, banks of snow were pushed up on either side defining our passage through the pass. We tried to avoid the big trucks spraying slush, rocks and mush on this clear, sunny day. Avoiding more windshield pits took some maneuvering and resulted in many fingerprints on the glass as we held to the belief that our hands on the glass could prevent a chipping disaster.

I like to navigate and am usually pretty good at it if I do say so myself. It's not that we need much navigation, knowing that one can go all the way from Canada to L.A. on Interstate 5. The truth is, I love maps. I love having the bigger picture embedded with all the small details. Maps, when they're well made and accurate, of course, are my dear friends. My current favorite is an atlas made for truckers that has laminated indestructible pages. No amount of use seems to phase it in the least. Unlike a road atlas for common mortals, this one for truckers has big, readable, laminated page maps and details – details I never could have imagined that I might need, or frankly, never do need. Yet, these details have increased my travel need quotient for details considerably. I carry this truckers' atlas with me on all my road trips.

After we cleared the pass and started the easy descent, I pulled out "the atlas."

"Let's see where we are." I said. "And see if we have any more passes while we're coping with this front." We had seen on the weather report the night before that there was a possibility that a heavy storm front would be stretching from the Oregon-California border in the north to Los Angeles in the south. I was hoping that our passage on Interstate 5 wouldn't involve too many mountain passes if we had to deal with such a large and intense storm front. A quick glance at the map immediately told me that we had not cleared all our passes and would have more mountains ahead of us.

Since Pete, my manager, was driving, I had time for map play and I decided that I needed to locate us in time and space – for myself, of course.

"So, you've never been to the Redwoods?" I asked for the umpteenth time. I found it incredulous that Pete, who had traveled so much and traveled with me so much, had never been to the Redwoods – any Redwoods. I, on the other hand, was intimate with every patch of Redwoods, great or small, that was in any way legally (or sometimes not legally) accessible.

To say I love the Redwoods is so flat, so unimbued with my reality as to be almost recklessly meaningless. I love the Redwoods like a familiar lover who knows all the folds and flows of my body, tenderly reaching out to stroke back life into hidden places that have gone untouched by daily living. I love the Redwoods because I know the presence of God in a unique way when they encircle me with a meditative stillness that eagerly listens for my soul to speak. I love the Redwoods for having seen a history in their rings of growth and holding it in majestic silence to transmit it to those who risk opening their soul to hearing what we can never know. I love the Redwoods because the silence of their standing movement heals wounds I have yet to comprehend. I love the Redwoods because they never cease to remind me of the alive fullness I feel in being a lover and having that love infinited back to me. I love the Redwoods, for in the Redwoods, I have no question about the practice of the presence of God in all my comings and goings. For me, the Redwoods and the nearness of God are one and the same. I love the Redwoods.

How could someone so close to me not know the Redwoods? They are as integral to my essence as life itself. To know me must mean to know the Redwoods. Pete must just mean that he hasn't met them in person yet.

With the knowledge of a "Redwood non-knowing" person sitting in the car next to me, I started scouring the map trying to spot the nearest Redwood grove. Maybe there was an accessible stand of Redwoods near enough to the highway that we could make a small detour. We were in a hurry and I know that "The practical shall always be in the service of the important," so I looked for Redwoods.

Then, I spotted it – The Klamath River! Yreka and Eureka! – the towns that were for me the beginning of the Klamath River Road. Seventy-five years melted into nothing as I gently put my fingers on the map and traced the road along the Klamath River as if the map could transmit memories through mere touch. A flood of images infused my being as my fingers moved slowly, carefully along the line of the river . . . Happy Camp . . . Clear Creek . . . Eureka. The tug of the Klamath River was so strong for me that when we breezed by the turnoff for the river, speeding straight down Interstate 5, I felt my body pulled so intensely to the right, down the ramp, away from the Interstate, and onto the Klamath River Road that I found myself dazed in disbelief that the green Range Rover had continued straight ahead down the interstate.

It was then that I knew, as I approached eighty-years-old, the time had come to share a history and experiences no longer known or even imagined. As I said, my father had dictated and I had transcribed his memories of that trip, that brave and precious adventure. Even the fact that we did what we did when we did it at all says so much about my family, who we were, and how we encountered, embraced, and plunged into life. And, even more importantly, it is a story and a history about a time and place that is no more. It is about ordinary people who lived extraordinary lives while being extraordinary people living lives that were ordinary in that time in history. It is about the lives and souls of a people and of a place inextricably intertwined in their separateness. These Tales of the Klamath are the real life adventures of a family that dared to live fully. These memories, so vivid and clear, transport us to people and lives not even imaged or thought about in today's world, yet precious in their existence. Unlike grave markers, these memories are the living testimony of a land and a people who deserve to be remembered the way they were.

I have my father's memory of the trip, dictated before he died. I have the clear and amazingly vivid, still sensory memory of a barely five-year-old, toe-headed blonde, little girl who lived in cowboy boots (my feet were too narrow for the children's shoes available in 1939), my "cowgirl costume" sewn out of black and white cotton, patterned to look like the skin of a paint horse or a Holstein cow and fringed around the knees. My cowgirl costume consisted of a short, knee-length culotte shirt with a matching vest and, along with a six-shooter holster and belt, was a birthday present from my mother for my fifth birthday shortly before we left to go gold mining. My six-shooter was slung on my left hip facing backwards so I could easily reach across with my right hand, after some practice, being able to twirl it and be ready for action. I still have the cowgirl outfit.

And then, there is the memory and perception of the woman I have become who has lived much and well with my eighty-three-year-old perceptions, who has studied others and studied herself, observed family patterns and raised her own family, worked with people who were so controlled that they were afraid to allow any change in their routine and those whose impulsive, restless abandon fractured their lives and that of those around them. I have looked deeply into others and myself, lived intensely in nature and drunk happily and painfully of life, its simplicity and its complexity and I treasure all its aspects. These "tales" then, will be an interweaving of that little girl, that woman and the man who shaped her life as her father as well as those memories shared in loving musings with her long dead mother over the years as we looked back together over this time.

Perhaps that time and those people will, then, never be forgotten and the history and lives of the people of the Ozarks and those of the Klamath River in California can be a part of those who knew someone, who knew someone, who knew someone who knew another way, in another time, and will bring forward a wisdom sorely needed of roots and lives and ways of being with all life.

# PART I

# THE WOMB

The year was 1937. It was spring and I had just turned three. The redbuds and dogwoods were rioting beauty over the hillsides and tiny spring flowers were carefully opening in the new, pale green meadows. You know, as I said, I think the prettiest sight I have ever seen is looking across a gully at a hillside of dogwoods in full bloom. The trunks of the dogwoods are very dark, thin, spindly and almost invisible. When the trees are blooming, it's like a garden of floating flower canopies suspended in mid-air. Those trees in bloom in the spring are magical, ethereal islands of blooms. Then, punctuate them with redbuds so profoundly pink that you can't believe color like that really exists and the tender, delicate green hills are transformed into a wonderland.

Grandma Reed told me a story about the dogwood. She said that long, long ago the dogwood tree was big and strong. It stood tall and arrogant in the forest and lorded over the other trees. Then, when they needed a wooden cross on which to crucify Jesus, they chose the dogwood because it was so straight and strong. After that, the dogwood was so ashamed that it decided that it never wanted to be used that way again. So, it vowed always to grow thin and crooked – and so it has. That's why you can't see the trunk when the canopy of blossoms are blooming. I also think the dogwood wants you to concentrate on the blossoms, not on it. Grandma said that if you look at the blossoms, there are four petals. Those are for the four gospels: Matthew, Mark, Luke and John. If you look closely, each petal has a place on the end that looks like a nail went through it leaving rust on it. Those are for the nails that were driven into Jesus' hands and feet. Then if you look carefully in the middle, there are little prickles like thorns. That is for the crown of thorns He wore. You can learn at lot looking at a flower.

At that time of our starting for California, back in 1939, we were living in Watts, Oklahoma, a town of about 100 people in Northeastern Oklahoma, tucked into the rolling, forested hills of the Ozark country, close to the long, khaki-brown colored, ambling Illinois River and just six miles from the Arkansas line. Rumor has it that at one time Watts had been a promising, little, railroad boomtown but in my lifetime it had become one of those places left in the backwash of the supposedly onward movement of time. One could even say, perhaps, that as the wheels of time ground on, Watts was spit out by their grinding and the expelled residue consisted more of a ground-up sand from the wheels than useable grain.

Before my time, it was, indeed, a hideout for bandits and highway men and women like Jesse and Frank James and Belle Star in the lawless "Oklahoma Territory." As I mentioned earlier, we had a great uncle killed by Jesse James. Jesse James was pretty respected where I came from.

Those of us who know Watts and have known it for generations, love Watts. We are like faithful husbands and wives who look tenderly at a fat, aging body of our life's companions and see within that person all we have known and loved. Strangers come, stay a while and go. Yet, those faithful to Watts stay or return with fond memories in their hearts for the place that has spawned us and the unconventional, sometimes whimsical and always idiosyncratic and easy-going people who nurtured us.

As I said, when my mother was a teenager, Watts had been a booming railroad town. It was the end of the line for the railroad and the home of the all-important roundhouse. When my mother was a young woman, life in Watts seemed to revolve around the big old, wooden circular roundhouse. As I was told, the roundhouse was the structure built to turn around the huge lumbering steam engines of that era when they had reached the end of the line so they could go back in the other direction. There was a railroad hotel where my mother had worked as a young woman. She had many stories about her waitressing there – the railroad men who overnighted at the small hotel, the joking and laughter, the fellow with the juice harp (harmonica) who would pull it out and in no time bring tears to your eyes just with the haunting sadness of the melodies he could pull out of that small instrument. These were happy days for my mother and Watts was teeming with life and excitement. (My mother was a poet and writer and a great storyteller. Any experience, no matter how small was worthy of a good story to be told on quiet afternoons and evenings.) The old hotel was two story with a big porch all the way across the front. The porch was concrete with concrete steps leading up to it and a stuccoed-over concrete wall that surrounded it with big, square wooden pillars going from the concrete wall to the roof to hold up the roof. The top of the wall between the pillars consisted of a flat concrete "shelf" good for sitting. It evidently had been quite grand in its day and probably the biggest and most impressive building in Watts. In my childhood memory, it was pretty ramshackled. The concrete had cracked and the roof needed repair and sagged a bit. Yet, whenever we passed it, I was always able to see it through my mother's eyes as well as in its present condition. (It has since been lovingly restored by one of those people such as myself, who comes from generations of "Watts' lovers.")

My grandfather's store was away from the highway just down the alley, a half a block from the old hotel. The store was a long building covered with tan, fake brick, tarpaper siding. Their living quarters were in the back. His shed and workshop abutted the back yard of the hotel. Grandpa Willey owned one of the two country stores in town. Before he opened the store, he had been a baker, and a very good one I might add. I have never found cream horns anywhere in the world that even come near to rivaling his. When Watts could no longer support a bakery, he turned his into a full-service country store. He was owner, clerk, butcher, accountant, and purveyor of all necessary items needed for survival and with an occasional (very occasional) non-essential whimsy at one's fingertips. He had large bins with humongous scoops in them, where he would dump huge 20-50 pound bags of flour, cornmeal, beans, sugar, and chicken and cow feed. He would then weigh out quantities people could afford on his marvelous scale. The scale was all brass with a marble slab on which he placed the bags to be weighed. I loved watching the big brass pointer swing back and forth as he carefully tapped in from his scoop just the amount his customer wanted. Then, he always went over the amount requested just a little bit and never charged for it, knowing that every family was just getting by and needed a bit extra. He was also an honest and good businessman and during the Depression, that tiny bit extra was much appreciated by his customers. I always felt warm inside watching the faces of the women who had carefully calculated to the cent what they could afford, becoming a little anxious when the scale settled a little over the requested amount. My grandfather would quickly start folding up the sack saying, "Ah, that's okay, just about right. You said you needed a half pound, right?" Relief and gratitude would move across the woman's face and she might even start to tear up. Before she could thank him he would say, "How are the kids doing? I heard little Clarice was ailing. Is she doing better?" Relieved with the change in topic, she would smile warmly and enter into conversation abandoning her worries for a few minutes.

"Now let's see, I suppose you want me to write that down in your credit book, right?" Again, the shame and sadness as her eyes slid downward and her body sagged. "If you don't mind?" she would say. Wordlessly, (for what could be said?), he would pull out the little receipt book with her name across the spine and make a detailed list of her purchases for the day, giving her the top page and keeping the copy in the book. The list was never long.

½ lb flour 16¢
¼ lb sugar 6¢
½ lb coffee 20¢
2 potatoes 07¢
¼ lb bacon 35¢

She would take the receipt and, keeping her eyes downcast, pack it into her bag. Then, just before she left he would say, "Oh, I almost forgot. Let me give you a jelly bean for each of the children," and he would count out exactly one apiece and drop them in her bag. She would blush and say, "Thank you. I'm sorry I can't pay our bill right now. We will when we can." He would cut her off and say, "Of course you will. You always have. We have to keep growing children healthy now, don't we?" as he ushered her to the door. I had seen the scene repeated so often that the faces of the women all seem to blend together in my mind. There were many of them and they always seemed to know to come when no one else was in the store – to save face – for everyone. Sometimes, I believed Grandpa and Mr. Waldroop, the other grocer, were keeping the whole town alive. I am quite sure that almost a whole generation of children in that small town grew to adulthood as relatively healthy persons because of Grandpa's and Mr. Waldroop's "credit books."

After they left, I would often question my grandpa.

"Will they ever pay, Grandpa?" I would ask.

"Of course they will when they have it, Elizabeth Anne. They've just hit upon some hard times right now like a lot of people."

I could never see how he made any money and that didn't seem to be what was important. He needed to know that the children were being fed and community always was more important than money. We, after all, had our garden, cows and chickens. We wouldn't starve.

That's the way business was carried on in Indian Country.

My grandfather was crippled from a childhood injury. One leg was much shorter than the other and he had a built-up shoe on the shorter foot. This didn't correct his gait and he walked with a pronounced limp, stepping out with his crippled foot as he threw his hip out and then quickly moving the other foot forward. I always thought he looked a little like a duck with a broken leg. It must have been painful and required a lot of effort for him to move around at all. He worked long, hard hours and I never once heard him complain. He would buy sides of beef for the store and then do all his own butchering. I was amazed how he could swing one of those big sides of beef around, plop it on the butcher block and, with a razor-sharp boning knife that he had just "stropped," turn it into steaks, roasts, short ribs and hamburger. He made the best sausage in the world. We grew the sage ourselves. His sausage ranked right up there with his cream horns. I was underfoot a lot because I always liked to be in on what was going on and everyone, even a little three- or four-year-old, chipped in and helped when needed.

My grandfather was also very intelligent and well-read. My mother would often say that if he had had a chance, he would have gone to college and had a profession. The one sacred time of the day when we all had to be very quiet and respectful was when Walter Winchell was on the radio. Grandpa would pull his chair up close to the large, old, wooden radio with the curved cabinet, take off his glasses to rest his eyes, and lean his bald head, rimmed with white hair, close to the radio so as not to miss a word. I'll never forget, "I'll be back in a flash with a flash." Mr. Winchell, which is what we called him, always said that. Most of the news was about what was happening in Europe (a place very, very far away), and the economy and Mr. Winchell always ended with a human interest story. These I liked the best. If we were quiet, we were allowed to gather around in a circle and listen with Grandpa but we could never disturb him. He was the elder and therefore respected. To me, he was Grandpa Willey. His name was Afton Eustace Willey.

Grandma Willey was Black Dutch. She was a heavy-set, roundish, plain woman who worked very hard. She compensated for my grandfather's being crippled and did almost all the heavy work. She oversaw the cows, the house and the garden. When a chicken needed to be killed, she did it. She had two ways of killing a chicken. One was to hold it on the block and chop its head off. The other was to grab it by the head and upper neck and swing it around in a circle until its head came off. Either way, she would drop it and the chicken would flop around on the ground until the life left it. I was simultaneously fascinated and horrified by the process. She then dipped it in scalding water and plucked it. I would help her with the plucking of the feathers. I would watch her and marvel at how killing it didn't seem to affect her. I now believe it <u>did</u> affect her and it had to be done so she did it to feed the four hungry "boys" she had borne to my grandfather, and herself, my grandfather, my parents and me. The hallmark of her life seemed to be doing what had to be done – without fanfare, without complaint. Almost everything we ate came from her garden and the animals she kept, augmented by the store. She baked all our bread and she usually let me churn the butter so that we had fresh butter and buttermilk from the cream saved from our Jersey milk cows. The churn was a big glass jar with a top that had paddles that went down into the cream and had a large handle on top fitted with gears that made the paddles turn. I loved the glass jar because I could see the process of the butter forming as I turned the handle. Grandma was a plain woman and she seemed to make every effort to make herself plainer than she was. She had a round face that was creased with the lines of a hard life. That face supported two large, dark brown eyes which, while they often looked tired and somewhat sad, seemed to me to be filled with a shy, gentle lovingness. Her hair was black and sprinkled with gray and she wore it in a plain bob blunt cut that ended just below her ears. In front, she either pinned it back with a bobby pin on each side or tucked it behind her ears. Her hair was something to be dealt with – that was all. It was never something to adorn or be fussed with. Her dresses were shapeless masses that slid over her head and hung on her as body covering. With a seam on each shoulder and one down each side – that was it except for two pockets always filled with something like keys, seeds or whatever she needed for her everyday work. The neck hole, armholes and bottom were machine hemmed. She could cut one out and run it up on the treadle sewing machine in less than thirty minutes. All of her dresses were made from printed flour sack or feed sack material. Her petticoats and underwear were made from plain flour sacks. We were lucky to have the feed sack and flour sack material. Since my grandfather ordered all this feed, flour and grain in big bags and then emptied them into the bins, we got the pick of the very best of the prints. The bags were printed with all kinds of designs, flowers, toys, geometrics, and scenes. Of course, they were made so that when we washed them, all the printing came out and all that was left was what we considered to be a beautiful piece of material. Mother always picked the sacks over carefully, choosing the very best that she could decorate with rickrack, bias binding, or pieces of other worn-out clothes and turn into something fashionable and beautiful for me, herself or my other grandma. Grandma Willey always encouraged my mother to take whatever she wanted and Grandma would use the rest for dresses for herself, shirts for Grandpa or the "boys," sell them, give them away or use them for dish towels. There was absolutely no competition for the ones she used for her slips and underwear! Her shoes were a horror. I was sure that they had been sturdy Oxfords sometime in the distant past but they were hardly recognizable as such when I remember them. She had broken the heels down by "slipping them on" too many times to count and the back of the shoes no longer existed for their intended purpose. The backs were bent completely down flat so she could slip her feet in and out as she chose – like clogs. She never wore her "outside" shoes in the house and always went barefoot or wore slippers.

My mother, who, like her Grandmother Reed who raised her, sewed her clothes carefully and always took time to have added tucks, lace, embroidery and smocking. She was always trying to give my Grandmother Willey something nice so "she could fix up once in a while." At every Mother's Day, birthday and Christmas, Mother would give her nice dresses, good underwear, a lovely hat, a "dress" purse or new shoes. Grandma Willey would always open the gift carefully, slowly taking it in with her eyes, gently touching her fingers to it, almost stroking it, and then would look up and say, "It's beautiful. You shouldn't have. Thank you so much. I'll just put it in the cedar chest for safe-keeping," never to be seen again except maybe at a funeral or trip into Siloam Springs to see the doctor. Mother would chime in with her usual response, "I didn't buy them to go in the cedar chest. I bought them for you to wear."

"I know, and they're just beautiful. I'll just put them in the chest for safe-keeping," my Grandma Willey would say softly. She was a woman of few words – with a will of steel.

Mother was often concerned that Grandma Willey devalued herself. I don't know about that. She adored and looked up to her husband as someone very intelligent and informed. She bore four sons and raised them well and she worked. She saw her life as work and she did it, plain and simply. For me, she was my Grandma Willey and I loved her and felt loved by her, although one could never conceivably in any way shape or form describe her as warm or affectionate. Hers was a kind of love you had to watch and listen for. It was deep and quiet, never on the surface. We never talked about her being Cherokee. We never talked about this with any of us. I was being "protected" to keep me from the boarding schools and no one around us talked about our heritage. At that time, it was much safer to "pass" if you could. And – we all grew up in the old ways in the important things and trying to adapt to the "new" ways for safety.

My other grandmother, Grandma Reed, was one of the most important people in my life. She was my great-grandmother, really, as my mother's mother had died in childbirth. She was my primary parenting figure in the first three years of my life. She taught me from the time of my birth – and probably before – for all I know.

Grandma Reed was a regal woman and a lady. Though poor – we were all poor and I didn't know that as a child. I just knew we were short of money sometimes. We certainly were not poor in any other way that I could feel or see. She always dressed in and carried herself with style. She was tall (to me then) and thin, not weighing over ninety-eight pounds. She carried herself with a majestic grace – body straight as an arrow and head held high, looking out on her world from a confident place of dignity. Her face was thin and narrow with years of life etched into it. When I came into her life, she had lost a daughter, a husband and her sisters. Only her son, her granddaughter and great-granddaughter were left for her to teach, to love, and to care for her. She had a long, hawk-like, Roman nose seated between clear cornflower-blue eyes. Her hair was long and silky. I used to love to watch her brush it. It was so long that she would run the brush through it as far as her arms would reach and then, she would have to pull it through the brush the rest of the way. Her hair was already silver when I knew her and it contained a yellow hint of past goldenness of years long since gone. She wore it in a bun held with hairpins at the back of her neck. She was the gentlest, most loving person in my life and she infused me with her love and her wisdom. I loved it when she would brush my hair. Her touch was so gentle, it felt like an angel's kiss. Probably my earliest memory is when I was a toddler being bathed by her. That was during the Depression and Mother was working as a waitress to help support the family and Grandma Reed was in charge of me. She would bathe me in the living room where it was warm, her hands gently sponging the water over my little body. Then, she would pat me dry with a towel – "It's not good to rub a baby's skin. It needs to be patted." Then she would dress me in my pajamas and I would run to the bedroom to the bed with the big feather bed, which she had already warmed with a hot brick wrapped in a towel. I would hop on the bed and lie back with my feet hanging over the edge and she would glide in with a warm wet cloth in her hand "to wipe the dust off" the soles of my feet. She never would use a wash cloth to bathe me. "Wash cloths were too harsh!" She used a piece of a very well-worn, old sheet. These "cloths" were as soft as eiderdown. After she wiped my feet, she would tuck me into the warm feather bed. That would be the last memory I would have that night.

Grandma Reed was a medicine woman and "doctored" all our family and all who came to her. Much of our time together was spent roaming the fields and woods, gathering, picking, cutting and digging foods and medicines. With each herb or plant, she taught me how to prepare it and how to use it.

"In nature," she would say. "We have all we need. When something makes us ill, there is always something to make us well again. Remember that, Elizabeth Anne."

My times with her could fill a book but that is not what this book is about. I will save these treasures in my heart for another time.

The others in my immediate circle were my uncles. Daddy was the oldest of four boys. Marvin was next. He was the one I knew the least until I grew up as he was away soon after my memory of childhood kicked in at about two-and-a-half or three. Francis was next. He called me "Blondie," and insisted that his dates had to be willing for me to tag along. On one of his dates, he took me to *Wuthering Heights*, a movie that is forever etched in my memory. He loved me dearly as I loved him. Then, there was Leslie, five years my senior who was more like a brother than an uncle. He and I had many adventures. I always went with him to milk the cows. He had taught the barn cats to open their mouths when he squirted milk at them. Both he and they became quite skilled at this. Of course I usually got "squirted" in the process! We grew up together. We swam, climbed trees, and explored ourselves and our world. He was Tarzan. I was Jane. He was Buck Rogers. I was Wilma.

One day, he and some of his "friends" were exploring eating some root of Indian paintbrush and he asked me if I wanted to try it. Of course I wanted to be included with the "big boys" so I eagerly said yes and took a big bite, ignoring the conspiratorial look among the boys.

As soon as my mouth clamped down on it, it was on fire! A fire like I had never experienced before or since. Thai, Mexican or Indian food – the hottest – couldn't hold a candle to Indian paintbrush. I let out a yowl that could be heard in the next county. I could see the panic in Leslie's face as my little legs tore for the store. Everything my grandparents did – water, food, milk – just made it burn more. There was nothing to do but live through it. Leslie got in big trouble. I felt sorry for him. I could see that he got carried away with the big boys and didn't mean to hurt me, and felt bad about it. I also knew that he had been tricked like I had been and his mouth had burned as bad as mine. We shared having a joke played on us. Maybe that is why that incident didn't affect my love and trust of him at all. Anyway, it didn't.

Marvin and Leslie were fairer, had curly hair and had a taller body build, looking more like my grandfather. Daddy (Virgil) and Francis had rounder faces, darker hair, and complexion and eyes and a body type more like my Grandma Willey's.

So this family and Watts were where I started my journey.

I remember Watts as a safe, gentle place. The park, had a long-since non-functional, tiered, Ozark rock fountain, and an aging bandstand was cattycorner from my grandparent's store. It seemed large and spacious and was perfect for hide-and-seek – especially in early evenings when the lightning bugs came out and filled the heavy summer air with magic candles.

The city hall, made out of the same pitted Ozark rock, stood at the top of the hill of the sloped park at the corner away from my grandparent's store. Large oaks and cottonwoods, with trunks that could hide a child, dotted the park. On the same side of the street as my Grandfather's store, the sidewalk ended at the alley that bordered his store. We only had two blocks of sidewalk in Watts and this was one of them. Often, several of us kids would load into a wagon at the top of the hill and fly down the sidewalk. The only problem was that the sidewalk ended abruptly with a broken drop-off at the alley. Amidst the thrill of our catapulting down the hill with screams and giggles, we had to make the decision whether to start dragging our feet midway down and significantly reduce our speed so as not to fly off the precipice or "risk it" and throw caution to the wind, prolonging the thrill. This, alas, was the level of important decision-making that confronted us daily in our life in Watts. As I look back, it seems that this decision with the wagon has symbolically repeated itself many times in my life since.

When I say Watts was a safe place for us as kids, I have come to believe that this early feeling of safety has been a major factor in my life and the way I have lived it. There was a gaggle of us kids that played together ranging from three-years-old to eight or so and growing-up together. We had the free reign of Watts – with prescribed limits, of course. We could go down to but not across the highway or anything beyond that. We could go into these areas with adult supervision only. The highway curved to the left as it passed through town so it was our boundary. Mind you, the "highway" was a two-lane dirt road. Still, it was the main artery between Siloam Springs, Arkansas, and Stillwell, Oklahoma, the county seat and points south, so it was to be reckoned with. My grandfather's store was a block down the alley from the highway. It seemed a great distance at the time and more than enough room to roam. We could go up to Main Street and the other country store, the Waldroop's, and the drugstore owned by Miss Nettie Ezell. I loved Miss Nettie Ezell! She was a widow lady whose husband, Dr. Ezell, had been long-since dead and she maintained the drugstore they had established. Most people called her Miss Nettie, but since I was a child, my mother made it clear that I needed to use her last name, too, in order to show the proper respect. So I was to call her Miss Nettie Ezell, which I did until the day she died when I was grown. Whenever I had any money to spend, I would head for Miss Nettie Ezell's. Her store had big, plate-glass windows on either side of double glass doors. The doors were tall and wooden with glass at the top and bottom. These doors seemed huge to me at the time and I loved just standing and looking at them. I liked all the glass and openness of her store. My grandfather's store was crowded and stuffed with just about everything anyone would need for anything. Miss Nettie Ezell's store was open and spacious. After I had absorbed my wonder with the front doors, I was ready to enter and what a world that was! The door handle was attached to a big brass piece, both of which she kept polished! The door handle was big curved brass, ending in a little matching upturned emphasis at the bottom. This brass curved handle was clearly made for a big adult hand to grasp. Above it was the key to being admitted to Miss Nettie Ezell's. There was a <u>huge</u> brass lever upon which adults could put their thumbs and press down toward the big brass handle being held by their hand. With luck, this magical contraption opened the large right-hand door. I believed that the difficulty of gaining admission to Miss Nettie Ezell's inner sanctum was somehow proportionate to the importance held within. My little hands could never grasp with the hand and push with the thumb at the same time. This door was clearly a two-handed job for me, which meant that I would have to let go of my tightly held nickel or pennies for a while in order to win entrance. Thus, my "spending money" was carefully entrusted to a pocket for a short time. If I stood on my toes, I could grasp the big brass handle with my left hand, push down on the thumb latch with my right hand, throw all my weight on my right hand, push against the door with my body at the same time and if I was lucky, the big door would swing open to reveal the wonders therein!

The inside of Miss Nettie Ezell's drugstore was always a bit dark and mysterious. It was cavernous and ran almost the length of the building which was probably about 75-100 feet long and about 40 feet wide. The ceilings were very high with patterned pressed tin. They were beautiful. They had grown a bit dusty and dingy over the years but I thought they were beautiful.

The store was almost empty. Long glass-topped and glass-sided display cases lined the front of the store and the walls and had very little in them. I'm not sure if Miss Nettie Ezell ever replenished her stock. I now think that perhaps after Dr. Ezell died, she just decided to keep the store open until everything was sold and did so. Some of the stock was absolutely ancient and I am sure had been there since my mother was a girl. No matter. It was the only other store in town besides my grandfather and the Waldroop's and they had almost all the same stock and my grandfather's was free. This meant that when I wanted to go on a spending spree on my own in Watts, Miss Nettie Ezell's was it.

It seemed to me that, for Miss Nettie Ezell, the store was more of a social institution than a business. After conquering the door and getting in, the first image was that of Miss Nettie Ezell sitting in her rocking chair by the stove. She was always dressed like a Victorian lady with her hair piled or knotted on her head. I loved the lace on her dresses always held by a delicate cameo. She seemed so proper and elegant. There were other upholstered chairs by the stove near her and she always offered treats and tea or something to drink (never liquor, of course) to anyone who entered. If my mother came with me, she and my mother would drink tea and visit while I shopped. The store was always cool in summer and warm in winter with her stove glowing with heat – all in all, a marvelous place to be. And, the most wonderful thing of all – she never rushed me. I could shop as long as I wanted and she let me "feel" everything. She would patiently pull one thing after another out of the case for me to examine at length. Of course, all of us kids knew that we had to be serious shoppers to go there, we couldn't just go there for treats and waste Miss Nettie Ezell's time. She was, after all, a business lady and our parents made it quite clear what our limits were. I never left empty-handed.

The same rules did not apply at other places in Watts. Across the street from my grandfather's store was Mrs. Carney's place. We all called her Mother Carney. She was the mother of my mother's best friend, Nannie

White. Mother slipped and called Mother Carney, "Mother White" sometimes because she had grown up calling her that. Mr. White had died long before my time and Mother White had married Mr. Carney who had also died before I was born. She seemed ancient to me and I loved her. She was the grandmother of my best friends Nancy, Carol Ann and Mary Jane (Nannie White had married Titus Chinn and they had three girls and later a boy, Alvin.) Nannie and Mother remained friends throughout their lives.

Mother Carney ran the post office in her house. She collected various varieties of hollyhocks and iris (we collected unusual varieties for her until her death) and she baked. Oh my, did she bake. The smells that came out of her kitchen were a marvelously tantalizing joy to behold. No matter where we were in our territory or free zone, when something was coming out of the oven at Mother Carney's we knew it and made a beeline for her place. She was always waiting for us with a plate full of something scrumptious. We all knew not to be pigs and made sure that the shy ones and the younger ones got theirs and we had a tea party almost every day it seems. There was another woman who lived in the big house with a huge round porch up on the hill who churned butter every week and if we just happened by, she would give us fresh buttermilk and cookies. We rarely missed her churning day either.

All in all, we had almost complete freedom to play and be children and the entire town looked out for us. It was a Cherokee town and that is the Cherokee way. Later in my life, I have reflected on how special and unusual that whole time was. For the first seven years of my life – on weekends and visits after three (we moved away when I was three and frequently returned) – I grew up feeling free and safe. I believe that this freedom and security gave me an inner strength and confidence which forms a core of my being. I owe much to that little town and the people whose lives graced it for a time.

## The Move to Muskogee

In the summer of 1937, my father was offered a full-time job as an appliance repairman for Montgomery Ward in Muskogee, Oklahoma. Jobs were hard to come by in those times. Our part of the country was still in the Depression – and there was no employment in or around Watts, so he accepted it. I know that it was difficult for both my parents to leave Watts, probably much more for my mother than my father as we had to leave my great-grandmother alone. Muskogee was a long way from Watts (or it seemed that way at the time) and a job was a job. I knew that they felt lucky to have a job anywhere. I had listened to Walter Winchell. Times were hard. People had to go to the bigger cities to find work so we packed up and moved, returning to Watts regularly, visiting and raiding my grandfather's store.

My father had no training in appliance repair work. Yet, he seemed to be able to repair or make anything. This was a belief I held all my life which invariably was supported by reality.

In fact, I actually, because of him, came to believe that the ability to make or fix anything was a sex-linked gene and every man had it. Unfortunately as an adult, I discovered that this was not true and had to take more responsibility for what he taught me. It was as if he had a mind that automatically understood mechanics and electronics. After the war started, he went to work for the Civilian Signal Corps and later, while working for the Federal Aviation Administration, was one of the people who did the early research and development of the radar used in aviation navigation (The VOR and Low Frequency Range). All this early research in radar was done without the benefit of a college degree or technical study, except for on-the-job training and a few courses offered by the government. He pioneered in electronic work – not through education (I believe he later greatly regretted not having his degree), but through intelligence, natural talent, boundless curiosity, and hard work. So, it is easy to see why Montgomery Ward did a very smart thing in hiring him as their appliance repair man. I believed this as a three-year-old and I believe it now, seventy-eight years later.

Muskogee was a big city for us. One of the first things my daddy taught me when we moved there was how to find my way home. I believe now that he was concerned about my feeling or getting lost in such a big city. He never mentioned his concern. As was typical of him, he only focused on the solution and made a game out of it to boot. Whenever we would go out, he would say "Okay, Elizabeth Anne, find your way home." When we first moved there, I was barely three and he would take me out for walks and "let" me find my way home. After we had lived in Muskogee for a while, we would play the same game in the car. He would stop at each intersection and say "Which way, Elizabeth Anne?" He would then wait for me to decide (traffic was much less in those days) before moving. Sometimes, he would deliberately make a wrong turn and I would immediately shout, "No, no, Daddy. Not this way, that way!" pointing in the right direction. He would smile a broad, warm smile with his gold tooth glistening (The gold tooth had replaced or capped – I'm not sure – one of his front teeth which had reportedly been knocked out by a wood chip when he was chopping wood.) I loved that gold tooth! Not many kids had a daddy with a shiny gold tooth glistening right up in the front of his mouth where everyone could see it! When he smiled that smile, the car would fill up with love and approval and he would say, "Very good, Elizabeth Anne, very good!" Both my parents took great pains to see that I was oriented in time and space and throughout my life, I used these skills taught me so early. No matter where I am, I rarely get lost or disoriented. In fact, even when I am in a place that is new and strange to me, I usually can go directly to where I want to be. In the woods or in the city, I have an almost completely infallible sense of direction. I believe that sense of directionality and orientation is due to this early training and the confidence instilled in me in the process of these "games" we played when I was young. This is the Indian way of teaching.

As I said, when I was three years old, my father had taken a job as a repairman for Montgomery Ward in Muskogee, Oklahoma. It was a long way from Watts, Oklahoma, which was "home" to us and also our first "leaving" of our roots.

One of my clear memories of Muskogee, and our first "adventure" in our new home, was "the turtle" we had rescued on the road. We were always rescuing something.

I remember we rented a big white house with green trim. Across the rear of the house was a screened-in porch with a concrete floor. This back porch was where we put the box turtle we had rescued from the highway on the way back from one of our weekend visits "home" to Watts, where we visited with grandparents and friends. Bringing home a turtle was a new experience for my three-year-old self, with much excitement attached. After we put him down, we all rushed inside to the kitchen to watch and wait for him to come out of his shell. The kitchen was big, going almost completely across the entire back of the house. On the right as we entered the kitchen, was a window that looked out over the screened porch. There was also a window over the sink but it was much too high for me so I rushed over to the window beside the door that had a full view of the screened room.

Daddy grabbed a chair and, without disturbing my watching, carefully and gently pulled me up in his lap. Daddy said that I had to be very quiet and very still or the turtle would not come out. I remember gluing my eyes on him as I tried to be the stillest three-year-old in Oklahoma and dutifully control every muscle in my body. I felt like I would burst because the only way I knew to be really, really still was to hold my breath. If he didn't come out before I had to breathe, I might be responsible for his not coming out and I couldn't bear that.

As I was sitting on Daddy's knee, he must have noticed my not-breathing philosophy because he quietly leaned over and softly whispered, "It's okay to breathe, Elizabeth Anne." I remember the relief. Not only could I breathe but if he had whispered maybe it was all right to whisper. Maybe box turtles didn't mind whispering. The questions started.

"When's he coming out?" "Is he afraid?" "Doesn't he know we won't hurt him?" "We took him off the highway, didn't we?" "Can he hear us?" My breath-holding had transformed itself into a million ideas and questions all pressing to be expressed before more silence might be imposed.

My dad smiled, readjusted his position as he shifted me on his knee and whispered, "Just watch and wait, Elizabeth Anne. He'll come out when he's ready." I heard this phrase, "just watch and wait" a lot as I was growing up. Being still and observing was highly valued as a way to learn in our family. Sometimes, when a person is busy forming and asking questions, they may completely miss seeing what is happening or what is there to see and learn. Besides, questions require your head to get busy. Watching and waiting requires your being to be alert. Again, this is the Indian way of learning.

I waited and while I waited, I watched. I looked at his beautiful domed shell. The designs were perfect – line within line, square within square spread across his house. His house! What a wonder to have your house always with you! No renting, no moving, just his house. I marveled at the way he could just pull in his legs and head and shut up tight – and he could stay there as long as he wanted! He was in charge of this situation as is often true in life that other people or other forces are in charge even when we think we are. If we wanted to see him, we were the ones who would have to wait! And wait we did!

After my initial flurry of activity and questions, I settled into waiting. Daddy never seemed to have any question but that I would settle into active waiting and I did. I became so involved in watching and waiting that I lost all sense of time and place. Nothing else existed except me, the box turtle, and Daddy's knee. We waited. With utter fascination, I drank him into my being. I fixed on him with all the intensity that I could muster in my three-year-old body.

Now don't get me wrong. This wasn't my first experience with a box turtle. I had seen them. I had seen them along the road. I had seen them squashed on the road during their migration season. I had seen them when for the umpteenth time my mother had said, "Virgil, stop the car," and she had jumped out and retrieved one from the middle of the road and sure death and deposited it in the ditch. Oh yes, I had seen them before but they were never ours! They were never mine! This one could be a pet if I wanted, they said. A pet! A pet turtle. My pet turtle. I could hardly contain myself with the idea until I began to watch and wait. Then, all was watching and waiting – and silence! I remember the silence. It was as if this was the first real thing we were to share – the turtle and I – the silence.

It was late. It was dark. Normally I would be in bed. Not tonight. This was too big an event. All routines were put aside as I waited and watched. I watched with so much intensity that I began not to see – or so it seemed because I became aware of a very quiet and gentle nudge from my father – perhaps I was dozing, who knows? I certainly thought I was watching! When I looked, the turtle was starting to open his shell – ever-so-slightly. I turned and looked at my Daddy. I was so excited I could hardly stand it. My eyes widened and electrified. My mouth was pursed for a squeal when Daddy's finger went to his lips to shush me. How impossible it seemed to contain all that excitement within my small body and I trusted that Daddy was right. Quickly, I looked back and the shell was opening wider. Daddy was right!

Then, I saw the turtle's head peak out – a little stub nose with a nostril on either side – two eyes right behind them surveying the porch just as we were surveying him. I was ecstatic! The colors – oh, the colors. I had never seen such colors – bright, yellow stripes running down his head and neck – even brighter than the yellow-gold on his shell. Then the dark green stripes in between. A dark green, the color of a wet hardwood forest in mid-August when the broad leaves have grown into their richness and opened to sweet, summer rain which should make things cooler and never do in August when everything is at its fullest. The gardens are bulging and the earth bursts forth, sharing the abundance of its bounty with those who are grateful. The forests seem lazy and complete. The rains arouse and wake them up as the leaves are washed clean of the dry dust that had accumulated. This turtle's green was that August green – green and yellow with a touch of red for emphasis.

Slowly, very slowly, his legs came out, bent at the knees with little claws on the end of each foot. He lifted his shell – his home – and he began to explore his new home – our new home. I was exhausted with the excitement and the waiting and watching. Both the turtle and I had a new home. I fell back against my Daddy and he carried me to bed.

This is my first memory of my new home in Muskogee. How wise they were to pick up the turtle, my new pet, to ease the move from the world I had known up to then.

We settled into life in Muskogee – commuting regularly back to Watts to be with home friends and family. Then, shortly afterwards, we moved to Fayetteville, Arkansas, where my dad became head of the appliance and repair department for Montgomery Ward.

## Lincoln Found Us

Before I actually start us on the trip to the Klamath River, there is one other important member of the family I need to introduce you to so you, the reader, can have a clear picture of all the individuals who participated in this adventure. This important "person" was our dog, Lincoln. Lincoln was a long-haired border collie. He was black with white markings on his chest and feet. He had spots of brown above his eyes and some bordering the white on his feet and chest. He was just the right size – not one of those "little, yapping dogs" as my father would say – and not one of those dogs so big that he could not comfortably share the back seat with me. He was the size that, when I was five years old and stood beside him, my hand just naturally rested on and patted his back. He was almost always right beside me. I have often said that he was my third parent and had a significant role in raising me.

Ol' Lincoln, as we used to call him (we had him for twelve years), came to us in a special way. My mother was always a great admirer of Abraham Lincoln. Mother (and my father too for that matter) always made sure that we traveled and were "educated" in every sense of the word. This meant that we often took family trips to experience history firsthand. Mother decided that we should go visit New Salem, which was outside of Springfield, Illinois. It was where Abraham Lincoln had lived – not where he was born, of course. Everyone knew that he was born in a log cabin in Kentucky. New Salem had been preserved as a park and historical site and it was possible to go in the cabins and museums and see exactly how Abraham Lincoln had lived. So, we loaded Grandma and Grandpa Willey, and Leslie, my dad's youngest brother, in the car with Mother and Daddy and me and off we went to New Salem to get educated and experience Lincoln's life.

As soon as we had unloaded ourselves from the car, walked across the parking lot, and entered the "grounds" of New Salem, this lovely black dog came bounding up to us. Of course both Leslie and I were thrilled and started petting him. The park ranger came rushing up and said, "Oh, I'm so glad you came back for him. I knew no one would leave such a fine dog as that deliberately." We all looked at one another with questioning faces and my mother said, "He's not our dog. We've never seen him before." The man's face fell and he said, "Oh, I'm so sorry to hear that." As we all headed toward the first building – with Leslie and me and the dog, it was love at first sight. The black dog proudly accompanied us from building to building, log cabin to log cabin. When we entered each one, he would politely sit down outside and wait for us to come out. Then he would excitedly greet us and walk with us to the next. When we had seen the whole village, we were back where we started and the dog was still with us.

"Are you sure you won't take him with you? He sure is a mighty fine dog," the ranger said.

"No, I'm sorry, we can't," said my father. "We don't need a dog and we don't have any room anyway," he continued, taking a firm position. Grandma and Grandpa said nothing and Mother looked grim.

"Please, please," I said. "I'll take care of him. He won't be any trouble."

"Ah, come on, Virgil. Let us take him with us," Leslie chimed in. "Elizabeth Anne just loves him," he added, knowing that I was less likely to be turned down than he was by the family since I was little, cute, the only girl and the only grandchild. We both got away with a lot because of my particular status in the family and he knew it.

"No," said Daddy. "And that's the end of it. Now get in the car."

The dog stood there expectantly wagging his tail as we all morosely piled into the car. I was crying. Leslie was crying. Mother looked significantly grimmer and my grandparents sat in the back seat enveloped with a heavy silence. Daddy drove off rather faster than usual and Leslie and I both got up on our knees and looked out the back window. The dog was following us! As we speeded up, he pushed himself harder. The road was dusty and we could see him running as fast as he could. No one said a word. Finally, he could run no farther and he stopped, in the middle of the road, looking heart-broken and sat down, ears drooping and head sagging. I can still see him in my mind's eye today and tears fill my eyes as they did then. Suddenly, in unison, we all shouted, "Stop the car!" My dad hit the brakes so fast that they squealed and the tires skidded. He threw the car in reverse. Through the clearing dust we could see that the dog saw us and he perked up and sprang into action. My mother already had the front door of the car open and when we met, he jumped in on her lap, licking her face as he passed, then mine, then Daddy's – in seconds. Before we could get our breath, he was in the back seat licking Grandma, Leslie, and Grandpa, then back in the front seat for another round. Everyone was laughing and crying at the same time, including the dog who whimpered and licked, licked and whimpered. When things settled down, Mother said, "We'll call him Lincoln," and no one disagreed. He was with us for the next twelve years and went everywhere with us so, of course, he was in the car as we headed out on Willey's Gold Rush.

Clearly, we belonged together.

## Deciding to Go and Leave Roots and Family

We hadn't been in Fayetteville long when old friends of my parents arrived back in Oklahoma fresh from gold mining in Northern California. My dad remembered it this way:

*Willey's great gold rush started, I believe, in 1938. It all came about because my old school chum, Vance Smith, had come back to Watts for a visit. That summer we were catching bullfrogs and shipping them to Kansas City. [1] He was telling me about his experience at gold mining up in the Klamath River. It seems that a company was formed down in Los Angeles where he had been working. The agreement was that the workers went up there and got food and lodging, of course, free of charge, and they would share in the profits. So the first three or four months there were no profits, because of the fact that they had a steel cable stretched across the Klamath River and to that they had tied a barge with a big gravel pump on it with the idea that they would pump the gravel and gold out of the bed of the river. Of course the gold had found to gravel. That didn't prove successful because the water was so swift and there were so many big rocks in there, they couldn't get around the rocks to pump the gravel. So they went back to*

---

[1] This was one of the ways my father and his brothers earned extra money, selling frog legs.

*L.A. and they came up with the idea – they had made a great big rack which they took across the river tied to the pulley system which tied to the cable system that held the boat in the stream. They dropped the rack and had a big Cat to pull it across. Well, they pulled out a lot of rocks, but of course, again the water was so swift that all the gravel and gold just washed right on down the river. So that proved to be a fizzle.*

What I remember of this time, was the excitement of Vance Smith's coming home from California. It was like the return of the conquering hero. Few people really left or got away from Watts, Oklahoma, and fewer still returned if they did. After Vance returned, there were many long nights spent sitting around together talking about his adventures, what the country was like, the wildness of it all, the people he'd met, the salmon and the local Indians along the river who caught them. I always was included in these conversations and could ooh and aah and ask questions along with the grownups. I usually crawled into my mother's or father's lap and listened until I fell asleep, waking up in my bed the next morning. My impression is that these discussions lasted long into the night.

My dad immediately swung into action on "the gold mining problem." Give my father a problem to solve and he was in his glory. The whole town knew it. When he was in high school in the 1920's, he had designed and built a movie projector from scratch from scraps and showed the first and only movies at the city hall in Watts. Until his death, many years later, when he would encounter a "problem," he would tackle it, sit in his easy chair, (for days if necessary), come to a solution in his mind – exclaim, "I think I've got it," and get up from his chair and head to his workshop to build a model and try it out. This is how he did his early research for the Civilian Signal Corps and the Civil Aeronautics Association. Many were the complaints I heard later in my life when "the government changed and tightened up and we could no longer build a model out of scraps and try it out. Now we have to farm it out, requisition a model to be built by some company and if it doesn't work, it's just a waste of time and money. I even have to requisition a screwdriver if I want one now. It's crazy." Perhaps this approach to problem solving and the curtailments and progressive restrictions he felt in working for the U.S. Government account for the four, stress-related heart attacks he had while working for the U.S. Government before he took early retirement.

But this was 1938. He was young and life was before him and my mother. Discussions led to ideas – ideas led to adventure.

As my father tells it:

*And then Vance and I got the idea that we'd go up there and do a little sluicing. Sluicing is when you use a great big pump and a big stream of water and wash it down and through your trough. They called it a sluice box. It is nothing but a trough with a lot of ripples put in it, which we made out of metal pieces of old cars. And they are bent in a 90 degree angle with the overhang pointing downstream, because any gold running down, being so heavy, would fall under the exposed part of the angle. But the sand and gravel would wash right on down. We spent quite a while and a lot of blistered hands cutting these pieces of metal up and getting our sluice box going. And down in the lower half, we put in pieces of rugs and things like that to catch the fine gold. So the pump we bought down in L.A. and, we have to go back in time.* [2]

*When we made the decision to go, well, we would go the following year, so our gold rush was in 1939, and the decision-making, planning and preparations were in 1938. During this lapse of time from 1938 to 1939, winter months, I bought a Model A rebuilt Ford motor from Montgomery Ward, and I had a good friend down in the machine shop and got him to make me a plate so we could set the transmission in backwards to get more speed out of it.* [3]

*We got all that done and I got a leave of absence from where I was working. We loaded a trailer down with everything we thought we would need – tools and the motor, my Lakewood motor and a sewing machine and the company gear with the expectation of staying out there*

[2] My father got a little bit ahead of himself in telling this story, which is often the way with storytellers, I have found. No harm – the listener is usually intelligent enough to put it all together.

[3] My father also made a trailer from scratch for transporting all of our equipment. This time of preparation was filled with excitement. Daily life seemed to step aside with the major focus being on our trip and gold mining.

*for at least a year. We had a camp stove with us and we*
*took a lot of canned goods and stuff from the store and out*
*we go – off we go to Californy-i-a.*

My father was a young man, twenty-five-years-old, my mother was a young woman and they had a just barely five-year-old daughter and a dog. Times were hard. Parts of the country were pulling out of the Depression and the Dust Bowl, and jobs were scarce and highly coveted. There would probably be a hundred men waiting in line for my father's job. Yet, he took (and they gave him!) a leave of absence and off we went. This decision, in-and-of-itself, says heaps about my family and who they were. Mother was just as excited for this adventure as my father was. They were willing to leave everything they had known, everyone who was near and dear to them, and strike out for parts unknown.

Our leaving must have been difficult for my grandparents, too. My Great-Grandmother Reed would be left alone – surrounded by friends and neighbors of course, but no family. Grandma and Grandpa Willey had each other and their three sons but Daddy was the oldest, the brightest and in many ways, the backbone of the family. Yet, the entire family supported the adventure, gave us what they could to help, and bid us a fond farewell. I find it curious that I do not remember the farewell. I remember the discussions and the decision-making, the preparations and the trip and I do not remember the farewell.

Mother would never say goodbye. She was very strong in her beliefs about that. She would only say "farewell" or "'til we meet again, another time, another place." That was the Indian way.

# PART II

# THE TRIP WEST

For any of you who have ever driven from Eastern Oklahoma to California, you know it is a long, hard drive. I recently drove from California to Western Arkansas and back again and, even in a Saab built for speed and comfort and interstates all the way, it is still a long, hard trip. I have an abiding love for this drive and even now, at over eighty, I would hop in a car, or, preferably, a motorhome, and strike out in that direction at a moment's notice. The land is so varied and changing and each phase has its own distinctive magnificent beauty.

The four of us – Mother, Daddy, Lincoln and I – left Watts and headed west. The land we were leaving was beautiful, Ozark country with green, rolling hills, clear, bubbling, spring-fed creeks with watercress growing in them, and vistas, heavenly vistas. One of my special thrills used to be when we would drive up on one of the higher hills (I thought they were mountains at the time) outside Fayetteville and Daddy would make a promise at the bottom that we could drive through the clouds – and we did! What a wonder!

As we headed west in Oklahoma, it wasn't too long until the land began to get flatter, less forested and less green. Shades of lime, chartreuse, bottle, emerald, jade, kelly, forest, olive, and hunter greens turned into tans, browns, grey-green, beige, buff, bronze, chocolate, dun, fawn, ochre, russet, sepia, terracotta and amber. Little did I know that we had left the green behind us for some time. My parents had always assumed that I was perfectly capable of entertaining myself, and, of course, I usually did so. Lincoln and I had a good time in the back seat. I had my dolls, drawing materials and clothes to dress up Lincoln when I got bored. He never seemed to mind and acted as if putting up with me was his cross to bear at times like that.

We also did a lot of family things as we drove along. Mother had a little book in which we registered out-of-state license plates. It was sort of like bird-watching but she was license plate watching. Of course we watched for birds, too, but that was just normal. Whenever she would see some out-of-state plate that she hadn't seen before, she would write it down in her book. She hoped to get all forty-eight. So, we all were constantly on the lookout for out-of-state license plates.

Then, there was always the history of the land. Daddy liked to know about the geology, Mother was intrigued with fossils, and both liked the history of the land from any perspective. We stopped at all the historical markers and because of Mother, never missed an Indian Museum. We visited the "good ones," of course. These were defined as those that at least attempted to look at history from an Indian's perspective. We learned about Longhorn Cattle Drives, and famous bandits like Billy the Kid (of course we already knew a lot about the James Brothers – Frank and Jessie – and Belle Star. They hung out in Oklahoma territory. As I said, Jesse was a hero where I grew up.) We saw the Red River Valley of the song, and tried not to miss anything of interest.

The going must have been slow with that old car pulling that heavy trailer over those two-lane roads and I don't remember minding.

I don't remember Mother and Daddy fighting on this trip. They did argue and fight once in awhile before we left on this trip. I knew that and I had heard them and I don't remember any on this trip. We were all so excited by the endless adventure that irritability and tiredness were always overcome by curiosity. Also, as we drove along, we sang. We sang a lot in our family. Mother and I went to the Methodist Church. Daddy didn't like church much. He felt that most churches were pretty much filled with hypocrites – I didn't know what that word meant and I was quite clear that it didn't mean anything good and I certainly didn't want to be one. However, I went to church with Mother anyway. Sunday School was fun. My friends were there and I loved (and still do) the gospel hymns – I learned all the verses by heart. Also, I loved the church potlucks and church "socials" like cakewalks, ice cream socials and box socials. Daddy never tried to stop Mother and me from going to church and church was quite simply, just something that Daddy had nothing to do with except for funerals and weddings. Then, the whole family went. So, Mother and I sang gospel hymns as we plowed across the country pulling our belongings behind us. We also sang other songs like, "You get a line and I'll get a pole, honey. You get a line and I'll get a pole, babe. You get a line and I'll get a pole, we'll all go down to that crawdad hole – Honey, Baby, mine."

We never used the word "nigger," in the second verse like it was written. Mother said nigger wasn't a nice word and I shouldn't use it. We substituted "feller" when we sang it. Mother said that colored people were just as good as white people and people should be judged by their hearts and not their color. She said that she knew a lot of white people that were worse than any colored (that was the polite word then) she had ever known. She thought that prejudice was an abomination and we weren't going to be like that. I completely agreed with her and knew that she was right on that one.

We also sang "Red Sails in the Sunset," "Little Brown Jug" and all kinds of songs. Both my parents often commented on how well I could carry a tune and what a nice, clear, loud voice I had. I took that as an encouragement to do more of the same.

But, wait! I've saved the best for last. The most exciting thing of the whole trip was the Burma Shave signs. As the land flattened out, those Burma Shave signs became more and more important to us all. They were fun, friendly, and familiar when little else was. We had many a good laugh with them. For those of you not in the know, there were not many billboards in those days and not much advertising. And, in the West, there were the Burma Shave signs. They were really quite simple and so much fun. Our speed made them easy to read. The Burma Shave signs were five, six or so signs in a row spaced just far enough apart so you wanted to see the next one. Each sign was a board painted reddish-brown with white letters on it and a single stick holding it up. Some swayed slightly. Each sign had one or a few words like:

"Is he lonesome –
or just blind.
That guy who drives –
so close behind."
Burma Shave

"The hero was Strong
and willin'.
She felt his face
and married the villan."
Burma Shave

"Don't kiss your girlfriend
at the gate,
love may be blind
but the neighbors ain't."
Burma Shave

"A nut at the wheel
A peach at his right,
Curve ahead
Salad tonight."
Burma Shave

The last one always said "Burma Shave." We always got a chuckle. We would spy them ahead down the road and everyone was on red alert not to miss anything. They rarely repeated themselves. We sure looked forward to those Burma Shave signs.

One of the good things about this trip for us was that we were sort of like our box turtle. We had our home on our back. Daddy had loaded the trailer so that on the very top was a mattress covered with tarps and a tent. Whenever we got tired, we would find a good camping spot – you could camp almost anywhere in those days. We had our camp stove and food with us so we would just make camp and spend the night. Mother and Daddy slept on the mattress under the stars or in the tent. I slept in the back seat to be safe and Lincoln slept under the car to guard the camp. Sometimes, we would have a campfire and usually we were too tired from traveling and just fell exhausted in bed.

In the morning, we would get up, wash up, get dressed, and Mother would fix breakfast while Daddy folded the tent and re-loaded the mattress on the top of the trailer. Before we left, I would help clean up the camp. My family always said, "Always leave a camp better than when you found it," and we lived by that rule. If other people had camped there and left any trash, we grabbed a sack and stuffed all their junk in it, too. This meant policing the area for bottle caps, scraps of paper or any litter. I can remember feeling good inside about my family and proud that we lived that way. This is a tradition I carry on to this day.

## Borger, Texas

Our first official stop was in the Texas Panhandle in Borger, Texas. My Dad remembered it this way:

> We stopped at Borger, Texas, which is just north of Amarillo, to visit – I think it was a cousin of Manilla's (my mother). Borger was set right in the middle of a great big oil field with derricks all around and the smell of the gasoline and oil was making me sick – so we only stayed – I guess we got there about one o'clock and either left the next day or the following day. By that time Manilla began to get sick from the smell of the oil fumes, too.
>
> The cousin had a big, old dog. Of course, we had Lincoln, and he thought he was the biggest fighter in the world, and I don't know as he ever won a fight. But anyhow, they got into it. Old Lincoln stayed under the car, and the other dog came out of the yard and decided he wanted to look the car over and they got into a fight. I was trying to separate them, couldn't make them stop. I hollered for a tub of water – bucket of water – to throw on the dogs. Everybody goes in and gets a bucket of water and throws it on me. I wasn't biting the dogs! Old Lincoln had gone limp. So I grabbed the other dog and started choking him, only to find out that the other dog had his lower jaw caught under Lincoln's collar – that was what was choking him. So when I untangled them, old Lincoln went under the car and the other dog went under the porch. From then on they were good friends and each stayed on his own side of the fence.

I remember very clearly my experience of post-Dust Bowl Borger, Texas. I was very excited to meet cousins who were new to me and approached the experience with great anticipation. I had never seen anything like Borger,

Texas, and was not and could not, I believe, ever have been prepared for it. As we drove through town to get to my cousins' house, I was aware that there was no green. The roads were dusty and anything that moved stirred up dust. The yards, mostly little fenced spaces of nothing in nothing, were brown and dusty. The only life seemed to be the wind, which blew dust, and an occasional scrawny dog. Everything was brownish-tan – the grass was tan, the weeds were tan, the dust was tan, the houses were colorless. I can remember a feeling of heaviness and sadness settling into me. If I had known the word, I would probably have described it as depression. I found it difficult to maintain enthusiasm and excitement in this setting and I put my arm around old Lincoln for safety and comfort. It seemed we all grew quieter and more drawn into ourselves as we approached my cousins' place. When we pulled up in front of the colorless nondescript house with the stock fenced yard, I felt a feeling of dread. With this feeling I felt disloyal to my mother and un-met cousins and never mentioned it but Lincoln knew and he sat very still next to me. Immediately, when we pulled up, they rushed out to greet us and we were caught up in a flurry of greetings, hugs and kisses. They had put a watermelon to cool in an old tin washtub filled with cold water and immediately they brought it out and cut it open. The bright, pink watermelon with its color and sweet, wet juiciness was a fitting antidote to the drab colorlessness of everything surrounding us and for a while my spirits lifted.

My cousins were loving and friendly and we visited long hours. Mother visited more than Daddy as they were her cousins and they wanted news of other family members. I wandered between the visiting and Daddy as he "checked the load" and played some with their children. No matter what I did, I could not shake the feeling of sadness I felt for the people and the land there. I remember the dogfight and I was terrified Lincoln was going to be killed. Yet, it certainly did offer some excitement and a break from the oppressive monotony of the world around us.

Our family feasted us with what they had and I remember my mother pulling from our stores to augment what they offered and subtly leaving "some of our special home-canned food from the Ozarks" with them when we left. I felt disloyal to Mother and family and I could hardly wait to get out of there. When we loaded in the car and old Lincoln and I were safely ensconced in the back seat, I put my hand over on him and we both were ready to go. I happily waved goodbye, sad to leave them in what was to me that lifeless place and relieved to move on. To me, and Lincoln too I believe, the car had become our home and our sanctuary. Neither of us wanted to be left in Borger, Texas.

## New Mexico and Arizona

Shortly after leaving the Texas Panhandle, we crossed into New Mexico – Land of Enchantment. My father remembered it this way:

> From there we went on, and across New Mexico, seeing country we didn't even know existed. We stopped in Tucumcari, I think, overnight . . . nice motel for its time.[4] Because at that time motels were just coming into existence. Previous to that you always rented a tourist cabin. Each little cabin was built separately, and you had a bed and cooking utensils and all the necessities for fixing and preparing a meal.
>
> Tucumcari, it took us quite a while to master pronouncing that name, but we finally succeeded and I haven't forgotten since. And now back to the motels. We stayed all night in a motel there. Somewhere along the road we stayed in tourist cabins, which was an individual cabin all supplied with linens and silverware and cooking utensils, but, as time passed, it got to the point where they furnished just the room, you had to furnish everything else, because everybody'd run off with the cooking utensils, the sheets, the pillows or something. I doubt very seriously if many people nowadays ever stayed in tourist cabins and remember them, but they were a nice thing for their time.
>
> Most of the time, we had the trailer loaded, and everything in there and covered with canvas, all tied down and packed just right.[5] And on top of that we

---

[4] We often camped and reading what my father said, I feel sure that we wanted to have a good bath and get that Texas dust out of our pores. We all had been affected by the experience of Borger. A motel must have been a big splurge.

[5] My father was a stickler for packing a load just right – load forward, heavy things over or in front of the wheels, balanced, every space filled. I often watched how meticulous he was about his packing.

*carried our bedding so we could pull off the side of the road, usually off from the road where we were screened from the road by brush, and made camp and had no problems. We just pulled off and lay the mattress on the ground with a tarp under it. We had a little gasoline stove which we used to cook with. Today, you can't do that because everything is fenced and you got high ditches and you don't dare go in any of the gates or the roads.*

*From Tucumcari, we went on, went through Albuquerque, old Highway 66, which in recent weeks they have had quite the deal on the radio and everybody has been talking about old Highway 66 going all the way from New York to San Francisco and I don't know what all. And you have the road originally started in Chicago, St. Louis, Tulsa, Oklahoma City and right on West. At the time we went over the road, a lot of it was not paved. Of course, we have the interstate going out there now. In fact, then, in traveling that country, it was wise to carry extra water and extra gasoline because you didn't find much water along the road [6] and if you did find it, it was so alkaline you couldn't drink it. If you bought water at the filling stations, which they had to have hauled in, they charged you a dollar a gallon for it. That is kind of expensive drinking. Too bad you couldn't drink beer. It was cheaper.[7]*

*Anyhow, on through Albuquerque. At that time Albuquerque and Tucumcari were only about three blocks long, four blocks maybe at the most. A far cry from what they are today. We crossed the Great Divide which Manilla was always worried about – going up the steep mountain and going down the other side with the heavy load we had.*

---

[6] Then, it was safe to drink water and fill our jugs from the streams along the way, especially in the Ozarks where the water was usually spring fed and pure, so I believe my parents assumed the same was true as we headed west. So they were startled and somewhat taken aback by not finding good plentiful water wherever and whenever they wanted it.

[7] My family never drank alcohol. They weren't vocal against it. In fact, I don't remember hearing anything about it. They just didn't do it.

*We had no problems because at that particular point we went over the Great Divide, we didn't even know it. We stopped and took some pictures. I think you have those in your black suitcase.*[8]

*Getting out into Arizona we stopped to take some pictures, and the state patrol car came up.*

*"Are you having trouble, sir?" the patrolman asked.*

*"No, we just stopped to take pictures," I responded.*

*"Oh, well, that's fine, I always want to help anybody that is in trouble," he said.*

*He was quite friendly, so I showed him the revolver I had strapped to the steering wheel.*[9]

*I says, "Is this gun legal out in this country?"*

*He says, "Yes, it is legal to carry it that way as long as it is in full sight." And then he added, "If you have to use it, don't hesitate to use it, use it if you have to." Again, a far cry from what we have today.*[10] *We stayed all night in the Painted Desert, got there just at dark. A tremendous thunderstorm had just gone through and there was still lightning and rain. There was a little inn at the edge of the Painted Desert. The road went right by it. So, we pulled off and thought, "Well, we can't cook, we've got to get something to eat." We went in there and asked for dinner. The response was "We can't cook in this thunderstorm. I*

---

[8] An old suitcase full of family photos.

[9] We always carried a gun or usually guns – a revolver and a rifle. All the families from Watts had guns (the old lawless Oklahoma Territory!) and most of the men and boys hunted to augment the family's food supply – rabbits, squirrels, pheasants, grouse, and quail. The women gathered nuts, greens, berries, persimmons, pawpaw. We always had fresh fruits, nuts, vegetables and teas from the woods and meadows. I learned early on what to gather and they were delicious. Everyone hunted and gathered. We were no different.

[10] My dad also carried a gun because he was afraid of snakes and sure that every snake he encountered was dangerous. My mother, on the other hand, was a snake handler. She even handled poisonous snakes and was never bitten. She became friendly with the curator of the snake house at the St. Louis Zoo and later collected rare specimens for him. I hated to have them sitting in jars in the back seat with me. When we would visit the zoo, the curator would take her down in the "pits" to see the new specimens while Daddy and I happily did something else.

*wouldn't go near that old iron stove." So, gee, what are we going to eat?*

*I say, "Can't you even fix us a cold sandwich?" which, after a lot of talking and wangling and all, they finally did and we took them out to the car. Manilla dug up something else, I don't know what all, and we had something to eat.*

*They had tourist cabins there. I think they had an enormous amount like a total of four – and, of course they were occupied. So, we decided well, there's this circle here, we'll just stay the night in the car, because we wanted to go down through the Painted Desert. So we all curled up. Lincoln and Elizabeth Anne in the back and Manilla and I sat up in the front seat and we slept in the car – which meant we didn't sleep late, that's for sure, because we weren't too comfortable.*

*Morning came, daylight came, we kinda waited for the sun to come up and we took out of there and drove around the Painted Desert. It is all different now. That same spot where the old inn sat, they've got a nice restaurant now and the road bypasses it.*

## The Painted Desert and Petrified Forest

I remember some different aspects of our visit to the Painted Desert. I suspect that old Lincoln and I were much more comfortable in the back seat than my parents were in the front seat so that part did not make as big an impression on me.

What I remember was the Painted Desert itself. When I heard the term "Painted Desert," I took it literally. I thought someone had splashed paint on it or painted a picture on the desert. I wasn't sure how that would be done, and that's what I thought. The Painted Desert was much more than my mind could imagine. Clearly, the artist was the Creator. There were huge hills and canyons with the most magnificent earth-toned colors imaginable. Brick reds, deep evening purples, terracotta pinks and sandy taupe tans were layered and molded into movements and precipices. The sight was breathtaking. I had never seen such colors in nature except in flowers and this was sand, rocks and dirt and they were constantly mutating and changing as the clouds rolled over and the light faltered and changed. The experience was like looking in a kaleidoscope but I was not looking in a tunnel. It was like I was in a kaleidoscope and the world was moving around me and changing patterns as it and I turned. I absolutely loved the Painted Desert and thought I could just stay there and watch and wait with it and its changing moods like I did with the box turtle. Those moments there when I was five began a love affair with that land that continues to this day.

We stopped at a trading post that sold souvenirs and I remember trying to find something that really was the Painted Desert. The postcards and those folders with strings of cards that unfolded as you held them up did not do it justice. The closest I could find after a great deal of looking and pondering – peppered with "Are you ready, yet, Elizabeth Anne?" – were the little glass domed things that were like those Christmas paperweights that were filled with fluid and when you shook them they made a snow scene. At the trading post, they had little domed things like the snow scene things, only they were filled with layer upon layer of fine sand representing the Painted Desert. At first, I was afraid to pick them up because I thought the sand would fly around and get mixed up like the snowflakes. Then, my parents showed me that the sand was in solid and didn't move. What a marvel! That was what I wanted. These domed wonders were almost like having a little Painted Desert all my own. Of course it took me some time to pick out just the right one with the right amount of each color in the perfect order. I believe I still have it among my treasures.

While we were in Navajo and Hopi land, we picked up some other treasures like a bowl, a basket and a tiny tourist kachina. We were careful with our money and yet, we could not resist getting some small things to show the people back in Watts. Of course we took lots of pictures, my mother saw to that, but they were all in black and white (which was the only kind of photo we knew then) and didn't show the breathtaking color of that land.

We also marveled at the Indians. They didn't look like the people we knew, the Cherokee, and they were all so beautiful and so different. I could have stayed in New Mexico and Arizona much longer and have since returned often as they became another one of the places where I am "at home."

Our next adventure came soon after we left the Painted Desert. We camped that night beside the highway. The next morning we decided to build a campfire and cook our breakfast on it. My family always appreciated a good, warm meal, especially to get us going in the morning. Daddy was fiddling around with the car and the trailer, which was not unusual, and Mother and I went out to scout out some wood for a fire. There wasn't much – some pieces of old sagebrush, some dead juniper, and other burnable looking things. Then we spied it – a big hunk of wood. It almost looked like it had been chopped off of something and it had the bark on it and everything. It was just what we needed. The other things we picked up would work for kindling and this would hold the fire.

"You grab that, Elizabeth Anne, and I'll take the rest of what we have gathered and we'll have a good fire." I rushed over to pick it up and when I curled my little five-year-old fingers around it – I COULDN'T LIFT IT! It really threw me off balance and I almost fell over with the surprise.

"Mother look!" I said, eyes bulging. She rushed over, dropped our stash of wood and picked it up.

"Oh my goodness," she said, "It's petrified wood." I knew what petrified wood was because we were going to visit the Petrified Forest next and my parents had told me about petrified wood. Plus, I had also seen some pieces and some jewelry made out of it in the trading post. But this was a big HUNK. It was so beautiful. The bark looked so <u>real</u>. It was rough and furrowed like the bark of a walnut tree. The "wood" itself was hard as a rock – it was a rock – and was red and brown. We could even see the grain and the growth rings. I was so excited.

"Can we keep it?" I asked.

"I don't know, Elizabeth Anne. We'll discuss it with Daddy." Then my mother's eyes brightened – like the light bulb in the comics we used to see over people's heads when they had ideas. She leaned down and whispered to me in a very conspiratorial fashion.

"Let's play a joke on Daddy."[11] "We'll put the piece of petrified wood in with the other wood and ask Daddy to build the fire," she said. What fun! I was so excited but I tried to keep a straight face as we headed back to camp with Mother carrying the petrified wood chunk covered over by pieces of sagebrush and other things. I padded along with my contributions of "wood" for the fire.

"We found some wood," Mother said. "Would you mind starting the fire while I get out what we need for breakfast?" He grunted and grabbed

---

[11] My family was very big on harmless, practical jokes.

the gasoline can to make his job easier. Meanwhile, Mother and I were giving each other high signs with our eyes and coming close to exploding.

Here's my daddy's version of that incident.

> *Anyway, we decided to go on down the Painted Desert a little bit and we'd build a little campfire, rest a little bit and cook breakfast. Well, wood was a little scarce out there. All of a sudden, some that I picked up that Manilla gave me was awful heavy. She had some petrified wood. And that sure doesn't burn or make a very good fire. But anyhow, we got something for breakfast. I don't recall what but something and went down through the Petrified Forest – much more interesting than it is now – more to see, I think. Maybe that is because I've seen it a couple of times. We looked at picture rock,[12] and took a picture of it. I think you have that in black and white, with all the pictographs on it. At that time you could walk right down and look at it real close. Now, it has been kind of fenced off with a railing. It has been defaced, mashed, scratched, chipped, painted and everything else. I just don't understand that in people.[13]*

Mother and I stopped what we were doing and watched Daddy starting to build the fire. If he hadn't been so busy with what he was doing, he would have seen that we were completely focused on watching him. He took some scrap paper and wadded it up, then piled some of the kindling on it, put a little gasoline on it and lighted it. He added a few more of the smaller pieces and then reached for the big piece, the petrified wood. We didn't move a muscle and held our breaths. His hand went around it and as he started to lift it, he said, "What the . . ." and we convulsed. He looked up sheepishly.

---

[12] A rock with rock art, petroglyphs and pictographs and paintings on it.

[13] My parents were always very strong in protecting the land and especially any "special" places like national parks or things like picture rock. They would always explain to me how important it was to protect them and keep them as they were found so that future generations would be able to see them and enjoy them as we had.

For me, picture rock was the beginning of a lifelong fascination and study of aboriginal rock art throughout the world.

We had tricked him. Our joke had worked. We were delighted. It was not easy to fool Daddy. We all had a good laugh and then examined the piece carefully.

"Can we keep it, Daddy?" I asked.

"What do you think, Virgil?" Mother asked.

"Well," said my dad. "We know we aren't supposed to take it if it is within the boundaries of the National Park. If everyone did that, there wouldn't be anything left for those who come after us to see." We all nodded in agreement. There was no disputing this fact.

"I don't think we are in the park boundaries here," Mother said. "We left the Painted Desert. I remember the sign and I don't think we have crossed the boundary of the Petrified Forest. I think this is open land between. What do you think, Elizabeth Anne?"

"Well," I drawled out slowly. "I sure would like to have it and I know that it's not right to take it if it is in one of those places where we aren't supposed to take it."

"What do you think, Manilla?"

"I think we are between the places designated as parks," she said. "So do I," said Daddy. "Let's check the map and if we are sure, we can keep it."

I was sure relieved when a few miles down the road we saw the sign, "Entering the Petrified Forest." We were safe to keep our piece of petrified wood.

I am so grateful for the way my parents taught me to respect the land and be concerned for the generations to come. These lessons are etched deep in my soul.

## On To California

I don't remember much of the rest of the trip to California and my father had this to say.

*We had another stop out in Arizona there or Nevada, I don't know. We were cooking supper that night in the sand. We had an open fire. I think we had run out of white gasoline, and hadn't been able to get any. I don't know the reason now, but anyway, we had eggs and something all scrambled up when the wind came up. So along with the eggs we had a lot of sand. We couldn't eat it and dumped it and started all over again. We had never seen so much sand and dirt blowing around before this trip.*

# PART III

# THE CALIFORNIA EXPERIENCE

### The Grapes of Wrath and the Border Crossing

My father had forgotten this next piece in the first telling of this story and I think it is important historically as well as what it says about him and our trip.

> This trip out there was made right after, a couple three years after the Dust Bowl, and of course everybody was going out there and people didn't want 'em. [14]
>
> I believe Steinbeck wrote *The Grapes of Wrath*, and while he was a great writer, he did a great injustice to some human people, because most of the people who went out there had enormous land holdings out in Western Oklahoma, Southeastern Colorado and some in New Mexico. For three or four years they had no rain there and the soil was just blown away. They tried to hold on

---

[14] The Dust Bowl affected parts of Oklahoma, Texas, Kansas, Nebraska, Colorado and New Mexico and was a time of prolonged drought when the topsoil of thousands and thousands of acres of farmland was literally blown away, forcing many people from their homes and formerly prosperous farms. It is believed that the extensive farming and tearing up of the soil itself also contributed to this national disaster.

and stayed until they had nothing left. So what could they do? California was going great in doing up its vegetables and fruit orchards and all. It was just the beginning of them and they needed help. So they thought, this is the place to go to get a job. And when they got out there, they were treated like scum of the earth. I haven't thought much of Steinbeck or much of the California farmer since because of those good people. The Grapes of Wrath depicted conditions, certain moral conditions, that just did not exist. If it had been in reverse, the California farmers would have been back in our area looking for work in the wheat fields during harvest time. Of course in those days we didn't have combines. You had your old mowing machine, you stacked it in shocks, you stacked the shocks in a stack and later on, a thrashing machine would come along. These shocks would have to be hauled to the thrashing machine and we'd thrash that way. There were summers back home, all the boys, except me, I was never allowed to do that, would go out to Western Oklahoma or Western Texas and work the wheat harvest all the way up to the Canadian line and come home again at the end of the summer with money jingling in their pockets. But I guess it was all right. I got along anyway.

Now, beings that I have interrupted my train of thought, there was one incident. I think I mentioned it before and didn't finish it. When in California, yeah it was when I got to talking about The Grapes of Wrath, the people going to California.

As we entered the inspection station in California along somewhere about Needles, I think it was, on that road anyway, people had been turned back. They were supposed to have so much money and this and that and the other. I don't know what all the restrictions were. They were turning people back, they wouldn't let them into California. So I go in there, for inspection, stopped and walked in there.

"Where are you going, what do you want to do out here?"

I said, "I'm going gold mining."

"Gold mining?" he said. "There's no gold out here."

I said, "I know there isn't but there is in Northern California."

"Well," he says, "We'll have to inspect your trailer."

"I don't care," I said. So I went out and undid the top and said, "Do all the inspection you want, there are no plants or anything in there. There is no fruit in there. It's tools, equipment we are going to need to mine with and household goods we are going to need to camp with."

"Well," he said. "You'll have to unload it."

"No," I said. "You are going to do the inspection, I don't have to unload it. You inspect it all you want to, but I expect you to put it back just like it was packed, otherwise it won't all get in there, and the load will not be balanced."

"Well, I don't know that I want to do that," he says.

Then I says, "Well, we can wait here until you make a decision."[15]

So we get Lincoln out and walk him around and kind of stretch our legs. Everybody was stiff anyway. He wanted to know if we ever hauled cotton in that trailer.

"You're from Arkansas," he says.

I say, "Yep, they grow a lot of cotton in Arkansas down in the southern end along the border and over on the east side. But I'm from Fayetteville," I says. "The University of Arkansas is there and I've never seen cotton growing so I haven't hauled any. Besides it's a brand new trailer. You can see that it has been freshly built and painted."

"Well," he says. "Let's go into the office."

They wanted to know how much money I had which made me kinda mad. And of course I had a chip on my shoulder because of all these things that had come back to us in Oklahoma 'bout what was going on out there. They didn't like Oakies. So, being from Arkansas didn't help matters any. They figured that we were one of the

---

[15] My father was a very mild-mannered man who would avoid a conflict at all costs. Yet, when he decided to make a stand, he was firmly planted. I suspect that he was also defending the faceless, unnamed refugees from the Dust Bowl whom, he felt, had been so unjustly treated by, rejected by and excluded from California.

dumbest states in the world and the other, Oklahoma, was the poorest.

So he says, "I got to know how much money you got."

"Why?" I said.

"Well," he says. "Unless you have enough money to get through here, that would tend to assure us that you were going to go where you say you're going, you can't get in."

"Well," I says. "I'll put it this way. You look – (I don't know the word I used, anyhow meaning that he was pretty well off, fair anyway for the times.)"

I says, "Well, I can guarantee you this, I can buy you out for all your worth and still have some money left over."

"Well, I don't know about that," he says.

"Well," I says. "You want to try it, I'll buy you out."

Of course I probably didn't have over $400-500 in the bank, and Vance and I and all the money we had together probably wouldn't even add up to that much. But I figured I could run that bluff. And then he wanted to know why I was going down to L.A., why I didn't go some other route.

"Well," I says. "There are several reasons. One reason is that my mining partner is there. We have to go down and buy a big pump and a few other things. And the second reason is, secondary to that, with the load I have, this is the easiest route to go. And the third reason, it really isn't much of your business."

Well they hemmed and hawed around there for quite a while. I imagine we spent as much as two hours there.

Finally, I just walked out and set down and said to Manilla, "Well, I guess we'll have to camp here all night." So I sat out there with Manilla and we fooled around awhile sometime more and of course every now and then everything was interrupted by somebody going through. They were checking plants, you know. We did have some too. I had forgotten about that, but no, that was when we came into New Mexico. Manilla went into the grocery store to buy something. We knew better than to try to take oranges or any citrus fruit in. When we went through the *inspection station, they asked if we had any plants, or this or that or the other. I says no. She says yes. I says, "What do we got?"*

*She says, "I just bought some potatoes in town."*

*"Oh," he says, "That's all right."*

*I think we did have three or four oranges when we were going into California, as I think back, so we ate them while we were waiting around there. I solved that problem. I'd almost forgotten that.*

*Anyway, he finally decides we can go on and gives us a little slip of paper and a sticker we put on the windshield or something and away we go.*

## Los Angeles

*And from there we come on West and dropped down to San Bernardino and took the road on over to L.A. At that time, it was still marked old Highway 66, but it's a secondary or lesser-rated road than the main route out of L.A. It's up next to the foothills. That whole area there from on into Pasadena was nothing but orange groves which have now mostly all been cleared out and it is solid housing from San Bernardino to L.A.*

*We stopped at this stand, they had cherry juice and orange juice – fresh – and we all got a glass full. Of course Manilla had cleaned all up and was all set to get to L.A. you know. And what happens? She spills cherry juice on her blouse. So that took some time, we had to dig through and get another blouse out.*[16]

---

[16] My mother, Manilla, was a very beautiful woman. She had a perfect hourglass figure. She was thin, had large, full breasts, a tiny waist and slim rounded hips. She had long, beautiful, dark hair which she either wore hanging down in bouncing curls or piled upon her head. Her face was clear with an olive complexion punctuated by a thin, straight nose bordered by chameleon eyes that changed from blue to gray – to blue – to green depending on what she was wearing. She "never met a stranger" and brought energy and laughter whenever she entered a room. Like my great-grandmother, although having little money, with the help of her trusty sewing machine, she was always chic and stylish wherever we went. She loved hats – the wilder the better. It would not be like her to enter the big city

*And we go into L.A. and find the address where Vance
is staying. He was at home! So we all had a greeting. Vance
had to wait another week before he could go and we had to
buy that pump, too. We looked around, went out to Long
Beach and got a lot of things out there and first one thing
and then another.*

Now here is a potent example of the difference between an adult's and
a five-year-old's experience. L.A. was completely overwhelming to me. It
was big! It was beyond big. It was enormous! I much preferred the hills of
Arkansas and Oklahoma, the desert country of New Mexico, Arizona and
Eastern California to this L.A. There were too many people, too many cars,
too much noise. It was just too much – Lincoln didn't like it either. He was
nervous about the car and the entire family plus, he had no freedom. He
had to be on a leash all the time.

So, both Lincoln and I geared ourselves up to be good sports and do the
best we could with a bad situation. We didn't want to ruin it for Mother and
Daddy. We were their "little troopers" as they called us. In the meantime, I
was secretly wondering if I could really trust the judgment of anyone who
liked this place.

## The Roller Coaster

Take the trip to Long Beach, for example. It only rates a mention
in Daddy's memory. In mine, it is a lifelong book. Part of that trip to
Long Beach was for Vance and his girlfriend to take us to this "fantastic"
amusement park. It was before Disneyland existed and was considered the
"tourist thing to do." So we went. Daddy wasn't much into that kind of thing
and Mother hated heights. She and I liked things like the tilt-a-whirl, the
merry-go-round, bumper cars, and things like that. I know Daddy got sick

---

of L.A. with stains on her blouse. She was a poet, a horsewoman, a gourmet cook
and a mother and teacher. Luckily for me, she was a terrible house cleaner so I
never had to live up to her model and no matter how short on funds we were, she
always seemed to save some of the grocery money for cleaning help. She loved to
camp – she loved anything outdoors. I secretly believed it was because she never
had to clean, although our camps were always tidy and organized. Nature was her
friend and ally – not all houses were. She was a healer of animals and people and,
I believe, never fully got over the fact that her mother had died in childbirth and
abandoned her to life.

on anything that spun too much. Anyway, I'm sure we were all good sports and we probably had a good time. I frankly can't remember if we had a good time or what we did – everything was eclipsed by the roller coaster. I had never seen a roller coaster before. It looked enormous! It had some horrible name like "The Killer," "The Thriller" or something even worse. Even the name scared me. I remember that. I think it even went out over the water. I have a faint memory that it was supposed to be the biggest and best of its kind in the world and Vance and his girlfriend were eager for all of us to try it. Mother didn't even consider it (heights, you know) and gave a quick "No!!" Daddy, who clearly didn't want to go either, said that he'd "stay with Manilla." All eyes turned to me. Vance and his girlfriend really wanted us to try it. To put it mildly, I was not at all excited about this roller coaster thing. My parents seemed to think it would be all right (if it was so all right, why weren't they going?) I was not eager and there was the family's honor to uphold. If no one else would do it, I guess it was up to five-year-old me. With a gentle, but firm, hand behind my back, I was pushed – led – to the roller coaster. Vance and his girlfriend chose the front seat so I would get my full money's worth.

I was glad that there were three of us in the seat. They put me in the middle, thank God. It seemed a bit tighter that way. I was also grateful for that bar that snapped into place that we could grab with our hands and hold tight. So there I was, roller coaster launched. The roller coaster started out and then began a slow, steep climb. Clickity, clickity, clickity – it didn't sound too sturdy. Being my father's daughter, I wondered how it was built. What if those chains which seemed to be pulling it from the middle of the tracks let go and we fell down backwards? I started a five-year-old prayer – "Please, please, please." After an excruciatingly long, tedious time, we were at the top. Oh my! We were so high, we looked out over the ocean, the palm trees – the world! People below looked like tiny specks. There was a pause (I suppose fully to understand the situation we were in), and then – boom – the bottom fell out. We plunged down so straight and so fast, I was sure the thing had completely gone out of control and we were going to die. I dropped to the floor with both hands still gripping the bar and waited to die. The thing shook and rattled, it savagely swayed from side to side jarring as it careened off the walls holding it, everything popped, plunged and peeled around the corners. Up we go again, not so high this time. People are screaming. I am beyond scared. People are laughing. I am nowhere near laughter. Vance's girlfriend leans down and asks, "Are you all right, Elizabeth Anne?" Who could ask such a question? Who could be all right in a situation like this? I'm in this rattling, shaking, plunging, little contraption with idiots! Survival is the key word here. Eventually the thing lurches and jerks to a stop and mercifully I and even Vance and his girlfriend are still alive. People pile out of the cars behind us and they seem to be excited and – happy! Can you believe it? What kind of people live in L.A. anyway? I am pulled from the thing and led to my parents. I am absolutely paralyzed and speechless. Daddy squats down and looks me in the eye.

"Was it fun, Elizabeth Anne?"

"Was it fun? Was it fun? You've got to be out of your ever lovin' mind," I thought. "Can't you see that that is crazy? That thing is dangerous! Next time you go and expose yourself to probable death for the family honor. I've done my part," I thought and I said nothing. I put my arms around his neck and he carried me for a while. Then, when he put me down, I slipped in between him and Mother and held on to their hands for dear life. I can understand why old Lincoln insists on sleeping under the car. My parents think it's because he's guarding the car. I think it's because he's going to make sure he never gets left again. I held on to both their hands.

My dad gives this experience in five words – "We went out to Long Beach." Can you believe it? That clicking, plunging, ricocheting, rattling, shaking, screaming thing erased any and all impressions I had of L.A. before or after. I just wanted to get out of there. The only possible positive thing I can now see about that experience is it was a lifetime preventative for adrenaline addiction.

That night, I told old Lincoln all about the whole experience on the roller coaster. He listened intently. Then, I told him how lucky he was that he didn't have to go on it. He agreed and we both plotted how we could get us out of L.A. as soon as possible. I stayed away from roller coasters after that for many, many years.

## Finishing Up in L.A.

*We still had to go buy that pump. So we were going through an industrial area. I think it was a four-lane road, it may have been six, but I doubt it. And we had to make a left turn down there. I was busy talking to Vance, and I kind of get a little far out and a police officer was standing there and came over to see what was going on. I didn't know what to say at the beginning. Vance said, "It's all right officer, he's a stranger in town and just wants to make a left turn. So he backed up and saw the Arkansas license plate on the car and he said, "Oh, I'll fix it so you can make your left turn." He goes out, blows his whistle, stops traffic four ways, and comes back and says, "Make your left turn." So we make our left turn. People were really helpful to us there.*

*Now back to going down and buying the water pump. We looked at several places that had big water pumps and we bought a two-stage centrifugal pump. The intake pipe was 8" in diameter and the outlet must have been about 4 or 5" in diameter. We had to reduce the outlets down in order to get the fire hose on. So we made arrangements to have that crated and shipped and we went on over to the Los Angeles fire department. They buy new hose every year, at least they did at that time, so we bought some of their old fire hose, which was good. We got that in a big pile, and I don't know what else we bought, not too much else, but we had to have them shipped by truck to Yreka. And, so after a lot of jingling and jangling around, we depart L.A. for positions, places north. Vance is with us and that was quite a trip. We were sleeping on the ground as usual. Vance had his own little pallet that he slept on.*

Again, the understatement from my father. We were leaving L.A. and Lincoln and I were ecstatic. Don't get me wrong, the people there were very nice to us. We visited with several from Watts and, of course, they were good people and it felt more like home and "good people." We stayed with them and they were glad to have us. It's not that the people weren't nice to us. They were, and we appreciated that. It's just that we were supposed to be going mining and we weren't even there yet. We wanted to get out of the city and into the woods. We wanted to get to the Klamath River.

Even as I am writing this today, I am having the same feelings, "Let's get on with it." It's all important information and we need it to understand our days on the Klamath River – gold mining days – and, as I write this, I can hardly wait to walk with my mind in those places and with those people of over seventy years ago.

> *I don't remember the area, but one place way up the valley there, we pulled off, late. It was after dark. We made our beds so we could sleep and the mosquitoes were terrific. You could just take and brush right down your arm with your hand and get a whole mess of them. All of a sudden, nobody said anything, we loaded everything back on the trailer, got in the car and took off again. Nobody said a word for about twenty to forty miles. Then, somebody in a quiet voice said "Sure got mosquitoes out here!" – which gave a little uplift to our spirits.*

## The Introduction to the Pacific

This trip to California was the first time any of us, including Lincoln, had ever seen the ocean. There's not a lot of ocean in Oklahoma and Arkansas! It sure was big and salty. I didn't like it much. I didn't trust it. Neither did Lincoln. He stayed back and barked at it. Mother and Daddy liked the waves – the surf they called it. They liked playing in the waves. I didn't. Those waves sure couldn't be trusted, I knew that. They just as soon knock you down as look at you. I knew that. They might be all right for grown-ups but not for kids. Mother and Daddy were always trying to get a picture of me or one of them with me with a big wave breaking behind me. They never got those pictures. I always ran just in time. I waited as long as I could. I liked to get in the ocean up to my ankles and play in the sand. That was good enough for me.

Mother was thrilled when she discovered the ocean water took away her dandruff. I was pleased for her if she wanted to stick her head in those waves. That was her business. She then got the bright idea that if ocean water was good for her dandruff, it was probably good for Lincoln's occasional fleas – they really weren't a problem. Anyway, she decided to wash him in the ocean. He didn't like that much. Not at all really. They dragged him down to the water. You could see his skid marks in the sand. I can still see his face as he stood there dripping wet as Mother gave him a bath. He looked like a drowned rat and he had a resigned, disgusted look on his face. As soon as they let him go, he tore out of there and rolled in the sand shaking sand and water all over everyone. Then he sped around us in circles like a racecar low to the ground. I knew how he felt when they were bathing him. I was glad he felt better afterwards.

Daddy sums it up:

> There wasn't anything unusual on the trip from there on up to Yreka, except it was scenic and all new to us. Probably got our eyes sore just from looking.
>
> When we got to Yreka, we buy a few groceries to take down with us and check to see if our pump was there and our hose and whatever else we had shipped. No, they weren't there. So we give them an address to write to and let us know. We give them H.E. Beck's, the man on whose land Vance had arranged that we would be staying and gold mining on. When the pump came in, they were to write us and we would come in and pick it up.

# PART IV

# COMING INTO THE KLAMATH RIVER

## The So-Called Road In

I'm not sure whether Vance had tried to prepare us for the Klamath River Road or scare us to death. He accomplished both. By the time we started down the Klamath River Road, our emotions were all over the place. We were wound up as tight as a grandfather clock on Saturday night. If we had been springs, we would have been so tight that none of us could even have begun to start unwinding unless someone gave us a little nudge.

We were told that the road in was a dirt road that was so narrow that there was room for only one car. Every once in awhile, there would be a wide spot and when you met a car, the one that was nearest to the wide spot had to back up and let the other one pass. We were <u>not</u> told that the nearest wide spot could be as far as one-quarter to one-half mile back. We were also told that there were no guardrails and there were great drops to the river below. The river was reported to be so treacherous that, when cars went into it, and they did do that, not only were the bodies of the people never recovered, but the cars themselves usually were never found. (This happened one time while we were there – that a car plunged into the river. They never found any of the bodies and only mangled pieces of the car "way down the river.")

Well! You can imagine! If Mother had dreaded the Continental Divide, just think what was going on in her head about this one! We had smelling salts and a little medicine bottle with a couple of swigs of whiskey, which the doctor back home had prescribed for her "fainting spells." She didn't say much about her terrifying apprehensions with respect to the road. I think she didn't want to scare me. In my mind, I was putting this road on the same scale as the roller coaster and trying to imagine which was going to turn out to be the worst. Of course I wasn't talking about it because I didn't want to get Mother worked up any worse than she already was. Secretly, I believe both Mother and I had determined to walk the entire ninety miles if need be (I didn't know how far ninety miles was and I was sure it couldn't be worse than the roller coaster). I had talked to old Lincoln about the road. He had, mercifully, missed the roller coaster but there was no way for him to escape the road. I'm sure he would have walked with Mother and me if it had come to that.

When we got to the beginning of the road, it was like the pause when you hold your breath before jumping into one of the cold, spring-fed creeks in Oklahoma. Of course, that was different because we were usually hot and after the first initial shocking plunge it felt good. None of us anticipated that this would feel good.

Daddy shifted the old '36 Chevy down and we started in. I think the rest of us would have been satisfied if we had driven the whole way at five miles an hour but Daddy knew that we couldn't do that and get there in time to make camp before dark. It was going to be slow enough going anyway. Whenever Daddy would pick up any speed at all, Mother would somewhere between a shrill scream and a quivering shout say, "Virgil! Slow down." Daddy would grumble under his breath and slow a bit. I know my mother's fear affected us all but she couldn't help it.

Lincoln and I chose to sit on the side away from the river and let Vance have the side next to the river. After all, he liked roller coasters! The river was roaring and roiling, thrashing and plunging as it thrust itself down the canyon. There were rocks and boulders like I had never seen before. Some were as big as our car! Imagine getting smashed against them by that raging river. It was so turbulent that it was almost impossible to tell the color of the water as it was mostly white. In telling us what to expect about the road and the river, Vance had neglected to tell us that the road was so narrow in places where it was cut into the cliff that the car hung over the edge and you couldn't see any ground when you looked out the window, just the river way down below. And then we had a trailer, too, dragging behind us. Fear had given way to terror as we crept our way along the trail that was referred to as a "road."

Just when we were making progress inching our way along, we met a car. Mother sucked in her breath so hard that the sound came out like an inverted scream. It was like an air hose had loosened in the car, "huh, huh, huh." I think she scared us more than the car and road did! Now what to do? We knew that the proper thing to do was for the person nearest the wide spot to back up but we had been so focused on inching forward, no eyes were looking right or left. We had no idea where our last wide spot was. Right at that point, where we considered that we might have to back up – <u>with the trailer</u> (and Mother was considering jumping from the car) the other fellow, clearly a local, threw his car in reverse and faultlessly charged back to his wide spot. You could feel the relief in our car – even Daddy – although I know that he was sure he could have done it. He was a superb backer of cars and trailer. I noticed my palms were wet where I was clutching Lincoln's fur. He was panting.

I think that experience of having survived the first car we met gave me a little confidence as we forged ahead. We did meet another car before too long. Unfortunately, the road was so twisted and carved out of the mountain that it didn't give us much chance to see the car far enough ahead to pull over in a convenient wide spot. After a while, we learned to pick up other clues – like sound or dust floating in the air ahead – and we could pull over and wait for the oncoming car to get there, which was what the second car we met had done. Everyone always waved and we waved back just like we knew them. There weren't that many people out here I guessed. When we met the third car, it was clear that we were the closest to the turnout so we had to back up. Without a word, Mother had her hand on the door handle and was out of the car in a flash. I don't think the wheels had even stopped rolling yet. "Come on, Elizabeth Anne," she said "and bring Lincoln. Hold on to his collar (not that he was going anywhere)." Vance got out of the car, too. "Coward," I thought. I briefly considered what we were going to do if Daddy, the car, and the trailer all went off into the river together. What if the trailer pulled Daddy and the car off? He wouldn't have a chance. Frankly, I think Daddy was relieved to have us all out of there so he could just give his full attention to backing the car and the trailer. Then, since we were in the wide spot anyway, we all stayed out of the car and walked around until we quit shaking. I believe we had a little snack and something to drink. We gave Lincoln something to drink. He had been panting a lot. I always shared my snacks with him.

Later down the road, we stopped at this beautiful spring where clear, pure water was gushing right out of the side of the mountain like a laying-on-its-side fountain. I loved that spring. The water tasted so good. Somehow, later, after many trips back and forth on that road – without a trailer! – I had begun to think of that spring as my "safety place." Whenever we got to that spring either coming or going, I knew we would be safe no matter what.

That's about all I remember about the first trip in. Daddy had his own version:

> So we started down the Klamath River Road. Was it narrow! It was just one way in most places – no room to pass, just barely room to get along the edge of the mountain. That is about . . . I don't remember how far, you can look on your map to see how far it is from Yreka to that town where we always went to shop – Happy Camp. It was mostly a forest service headquarters, and they had a grocery store. The prices were high. Gasoline was high, of course. They even had a moving picture theater which we never did go to one of the movies . . . And a few other things. I don't remember what all, not too much. It was a small town. You come in down the road and you make a big curve, and here it is way down over the hillside. And you make a big loop and come right through town and go right out again. That's the way it used to be. Now, Happy Camp is set back from the highway because they rebuilt and paved that highway.
>
> Contrary to the desires of the people, the politicians wanted to open the Klamath River Road as a scenic road, and of course they did pave part of it during the war down there. During the war, all gold mining stopped, but they had other mines down there.
>
> Anyway, we left Happy Camp and went down the road to H.E. Beck's place, an old log cabin, quite nice for its time. We could get down to H.E. Beck's level with the trailer, just a little utility trailer, not a living trailer as we speak of trailers today. It was a box trailer. The inside was the width of a bed and about, I would judge, four feet longer in length. We had it arranged that later on in life

*we rebuilt it and had it fixed so we could throw a tent over, just set the tent up over it and we had a bed in there and room to stand up and dress and all the camping equipment under the bed.*

*Back to H.E. Beck's. We were able, with a lot of trouble, to get the car and trailer down to H.E. Beck's level and I guess we were able to get down to the second level, the level above where we were camped down on the river.*

## Meeting My Friend, Mr. Beck, and His House

This is how I remember it. Mr. Beck's house was on the first level when we got off the road. The car and trailer were kept on the next level – a flat place – because of convenience. We stored some things in the trailer and carried them down to camp as we needed them and vice-versa and the car was much closer to camp on that level and easier to get to there than if it had been at Mr. Beck's home. There was no way to get the car and trailer down by the river where we made our camp. Everything had to be carried down a tiny steep trail – food, sewing machine (treadle), tents and tarps, sluice box, pump, hoses, Model A motor. Everything had to be carried or skidded down that path. Setting up the camp and the mining operation took a lot of time and work.

*Anyway, Vance knew Beck going way back to the early days when he had been out there before. We had friends out there who had been out there for a while too. John Thomas, from Watts, went out there for his health. He ran the filling station across from what had been the bakery and then was Dad's meat market and store when you knew it. John had taken care of his mother until she had died. He was having difficulty in breathing, because of fumes from the gasoline, I guess. When he just got out there, he said he could only walk about 100 yards and he was all in, but later as time went on, why his lungs cleared up and he was quite a hiker. Then there was Roscoe Langley, we knew him, he was out there. I don't know what he was doing out there, honestly. He was out there making a go of it. He married, I don't remember, I believe it was a*

*Stevens' girl. His daughter wanted to know if she could stay with us for a while, she wasn't much trouble.[17]*

*And another thing I want to say about the trip in. We stopped at a spring, and water was gushing out of the hillside all the way. Funny thing about it, you don't see water gushing out of the hillside anymore. We have been up and down that road a couple of times since then but the spring is still there where it was. Vance was telling us, "You can drink all this water you want and it won't make you sick, because most places you drink too much water when you are hot and it'll come up on you. This water won't."*

*We set up camp right down by the river. When we first went down there, the roar of the river was such that you couldn't carry on a conversation because we weren't used to it. But after you were there a while, the noise didn't bother us. We could talk in a normal tone of voice and we all understood each other.*

*The forest down by the river bank was such that we had a canopy of limbs and leaves over us and of course right across the river was a big, tall mountain. It was a kind of a bluff. That bluff didn't help matters any, because the sun didn't hit us until about ten o'clock.*

I remember pulling into Mr. Beck's place. I was so relieved when Vance said, "This is it. Turn here." I had just about had my fill of not knowing what was around the next corner with the possibility that whatever it was would be even worse than the last one and the last one had been bad enough.

As we turned into Mr. Beck's place, I could feel my fear and apprehension turning into the excitement that I had had for most of the trip, except for the last 90 miles or so. We were going gold mining on the Klamath River. We were going to live here – in a tent. We were here! I felt everyone's relief as we turned left down the little dirt road to Mr. Beck's place. It was just two tire tracks with grass growing in the middle. It was

---

[17] I'm not clear what time period here my father is talking about. We were always taking people in. That's just how people from Watts did things. Also, they sort of stayed connected no matter where they were. So we had connections in California and Vance knew Beck. That was all that mattered. Indians usually stick together. That's just how it is.

familiar. We had roads like that in Watts. The road was a little steep but not scary. We had to be careful not to hit high center. Lincoln and I could hardly wait to get out of the car. As we pulled up to the house, Mr. Beck (I always called him Mr. Beck as was proper and respectful of an elder. I had been taught how to treat elders. This teaching was par for the course for Indians. Daddy and Vance sometimes called him "Beck" for short.) came out of his house to greet us. He probably didn't have too many cars coming down his road so I guess he knew who it was driving in.

Anyway, he walked out on his great big porch which was pretty high off the ground and waved a greeting. I will never forget him or the house. The house was made of logs and was pretty big. He had built it all himself, even felling the trees. At 14, he came over the mountains in his freight wagon delivering supplies to the miners. There were very few "white men" there then, mostly miners. I believe the house had two stories. He must have found some pretty big trees to build it with because each side was made of one long tree after another with white chinking in between. I have seen log cabins at New Salem, Abraham Lincoln's place in Illinois where we got old Lincoln, but Mr. Beck's place was no cabin. It was a big house! It faced west with the south side looking toward the river. On the south, west, and north sides there was a big porch – covered by the overhang from the roof and supported by big tree trunks for pillars evenly spaced along each side. It wasn't painted. It was just wood and it looked like it had been there for a while. There were maybe ten or so big plank steps leading from the ground to the porch. I later learned that in the back there was a stoop that led off the kitchen to the back garden.

I'll never forget my first glimpse of Mr. Beck. He stood there with one arm up holding on to one of the pillars and waved to us with the other to come on up. He was not a very tall man. And I knew he was old but he didn't look that old. I had heard that he was ninety or so. He had on a gray, black and red plaid, flannel shirt with the sleeves rolled up aways on his arms and his long underwear showing at the open neck and sleeves. His arms looked strong. He had on a pair of non-descript pants held up by wide, black suspenders. The pants hung on him a bit and looked like they probably would have fallen off without the suspenders. His hair was salt and pepper gray and black and was sort of cut so that his ears were showing and it had a part on the left side. And his hair hung on his face a bit. His hair and face reminded me of an older version of Will Rogers. We liked Will Rogers a lot because he was one of us and he had become rich and famous. He was from Oklahoma and he was Cherokee. Mother said that he had a "home-spun humor" and he was very wise. Even presidents listened to him. Well, Mr. Beck looked something like Will Rogers. He had a kind of square face and he could have used a shave. His eyes were clear and kindly and he was bow-legged. I liked elders a lot and with one look I knew that we would be fast friends.

"How was the road?" he asked.

No one had words. We kinda laughed and tittered a little, as we were spent and uncomfortable. Vance introduced us and Mr. Beck invited us in to have a bite to eat and something to drink. We had arrived. I could hardly wait to explore every inch of everything and I knew Lincoln felt the same way. We didn't linger. We had made a very early start that morning so we could get there in time to make camp before dark and we had a lot to do. Mr. Beck said we could make camp on the first flat spot below his house where the trailer and car would be kept or down closer to the river which would be nearer to where the men would be working. We chose down by the river. It would be more work initially but less after we got the gold mining started.

## Hi Ho Silver

I realize that I need to introduce you to another very important member of the family who had been packed away for the trip and hadn't done much yet. Now he would be unpacked and take his rightful important place in my life. This important being was my stick horse, Silver. I rode him everywhere I went. Santa Clause had given me Silver the previous Christmas and since then he had been my constant companion along with Lincoln, of course. He was named for Tom Mix's, or one of the other cowboy's horses. Maybe Tom Mix said, "Scratch gravel, White Wind." I don't remember. All of the cowboys had a saying like that. We used to sit in the movie theater just waiting for them to say their own personal saying. We knew they would. When they did, we would clap and cheer and let out squeaks of pleasure. I believe it was like intimacy for us. It was like we really knew them and knew what they would say. Silver, who was whitish-grey, and I had adopted his "Hi, Ho, Silver, away," that he said whenever he wanted his horse, Silver, to leap into action and catch some thief or bandit. My Silver could spring into action just as fast.

Silver was made out of wood. The wood was cut in the shape of a horse's head. He had lovely hair-like swirls painted on his head to resemble a dapple gray. I knew all about horse colors and breeds. Mother had taught me. I knew the difference between a dapple gray, a steel gray and a flea-bitten gray. I knew the difference between a chestnut, a sorrel, and a bay and between a blood bay and a regular bay. I knew the difference between a thoroughbred and a Tennessee Walker. I knew a lot about horses and Silver was definitely a dapple gray. He had pieces of black rubber inner tube cut pointed like ears, kind of folded and nailed to either side of his head. I liked his ears because they were soft and I could run my hands on them just like a real horse. Sometimes I could put my finger in them to clean them out. His nostrils were slightly flared showing that he was alert and ready to go and his eyes were set squarely on either side of his head. He had a somewhat curly, twine rope mane and a leather bridle with reins attached to his head. All of this marvelous creation was attached to a long broomstick painted dapple gray, too – which I could throw my leg over and ride to my heart's content. I was responsible for his safety and care. That's how it was with horses. I was sure that Silver was eager to get unpacked from the trailer and explore our new home.

## Choosing Our Camp/Home and Moving In

So we left Mr. Beck, took the car and the trailer down to the landing – the next level spot – and began to get ready to unload the trailer. First, however, we had to go down to explore the area down by the river and pick the exact right spot for our camp.

I remember my first impression of the place where our camp would be. It was magical. It felt like a giant-sized secret place to me. When I was younger, I was always finding special "secret places." For example, one was under a bush in the front yard in Arkansas where I could crawl under and look out but no one could see me there. I used to take my dolls and animals and tea party fixin's Mother had given me and have my own private tea party. Another was under the porch. I had several. This was like a whole big, huge secret place. Our whole camp would be a secret place. I had never dreamed of such wondrous magic.

When we walked into this flat, clear space, it was a little past noon and the midday sun was as bright as it would get in our camp. I looked up and saw the sun filtering through the needles and the fronds of the evergreens, pines and the cedars. The light swayed and moved as it ricocheted patterns of light on the silent, needle-strewn ground. Who needed carpets? We had one that mutated and changed whenever the gentle breeze moved the trees. And, ah, the trees – the trees. They went up and up and up into the sky – not like the Ozark trees that spread out and sheltered you close, seeming more intimate. The limbs on these trees didn't even start until they were higher than most Ozark trees. Then, these high limbs reached out in a canopy of black lace, back-lighted by the sun. I would learn another form of intimacy from these trees as they moved and swayed, making never-ending light patterns on the soft earth. The trees were hypnotic. The sound was so gentle that it could scarcely be heard above the roar of the river and these two mingled sounds – that of the trees and that of the river, were to blend into my music and my lullaby for our time there. I was being serenaded every hour of the day and night by the trees and the river. The bird sounds were new to me. Mother had taught me to recognize most of the Ozark bird calls. It would take me a while to know these new ones but I had time and it was comforting to know that here, too, there were birds to sing to us and add to our lives with their presence.

"This looks like the right place," said my dad. Vance nodded in agreement. "What do you think, Manilla?"

"I think it's good," she said. "It's flat, it's practical, though not much sun. There's good water nearby. It's easy to get to the car and trailer and near to where you will set up the sluice box. I don't think we can do much better," she said. "What do you think, Elizabeth Anne?"

"I love it!" I said filled with excitement. "Silver likes it, too and I'm sure Lincoln will."

"Well, that's it, then. Let's get settled in our new home." I loved the sound of those words.

We all got busy unloading the trailer and carrying our gear down to make a home. The first job was to get the bedding, the camp stove and cooking utensils, and some food. So with a tarp to hang over it all, we could have a place to sleep and be able to eat that night. With this early requirement accomplished, we fell into bed exhausted after the road and the excitement of the day.

The men got busy the next day and made us a real camp. They made us a table out of scrap lumber and erected a frame over which they hung tarpaulins so we had our own little village.

My dad describes it like this:

> We had a tent to sleep in for Manilla and me – and that kid that came along with us [me!] and her horse Hi Ho Silver[18] and old Lincoln. But Lincoln didn't want to sleep

---

[18] Daddy is being funny here.

*in the camp. He was a wise dog. He wanted to sleep under the car. We had some canvas tarps that we stretched out to hang over a table we made, which was a dining table, cook table, and everything else was put on it. We had the camp stove and a wood fire to cook on. [19] All cleaned up, we had made a nice little campground.*

*Mosquitoes only bothered us about 30 minutes in the morning and about an hour at night. What we would do was put some green limbs on the fire and that would smoke them out. A lot of smoked mosquitoes out there at that time.*

---

[19] As I remember, my dad had made a kind of camp stove by piling some rocks around in a semi-circle that opened into our camp. He then put a flat piece of old cast-iron on it and when it was fired up with a wood fire, we had a griddle, a stove top to keep coffee warm on the back, and a great place for the old cast-iron Dutch oven. Plus, it took the chill off our camp on cool nights and mornings.

# PART V

# LIFE ON THE KLAMATH RIVER

## The Mining Operation

After we got the camp all set up, the men worked on their "mining operation" which was not too far from the camp by way of a narrow footpath that paralleled the river. They set it up near a small stream that came careening down the boulder-strewn bank and into the Klamath River. I believe we also got our water from that stream. There were little eddies there where the stream and the riverbed had cut into the bank and these eddies were like a mini sanctuary being protected from the main rush of the river. These still waters were a safe place for me to play and pan for gold.

I had my own small gold pan. It was just like Mother and Daddy and Vance's only about half the size. I believe we had bought them in Happy Camp on one of our trips into town.

Panning gold looked easy but it wasn't. First you had to scoop up a bit of promising looking sand and small gravel from the creek or river. It took me a while to get what "promising looking" meant and I still don't know if I could explain it. You have to be able to "see" it and learn to do that from experience. It does seem to me as I close my eyes and try to remember, that "good" sand had a kind of "black" look to it. One has to be very smart about this choosing because in areas where there was gold, there was often also a lot of mica (which is really a kind of glass, I was told, made out of silicon, I think). [20] Anyway, mica was called "Fools Gold" and it sure could fool you. It glistened and sparkled in the sun just like gold dust – but really gold nuggets and gold dust were a little duller than mica as I remember.

Anyway, as I said, you put a bit of sand and small gravel in the pan and then you tip the edge of the pan and quick dip a bit of water into the pan – careful – not too much or it won't work right, not too little or it won't "pan." And don't tip it too much or all your good black sand and probable gold will spill out to the bottom with the water, leaving you nothing to pan. I know all these possible mistakes because I made every one of them, many times, as I was trying to learn to pan gold. Then, you begin to swirl it around in a kind of rocking motion keeping the water and the sand and gravel moving so the gold, which is heavier, will drop to the bottom and kind of separate. My mother, Daddy and Vance taught me the rudiments but it was Frenchy who really taught me how to become a skilled "panner." More about him later, he was an expert on just about everything when it came to gold mining.

I actually panned some dust and a very few, very small "nuggets" (which were really more like flecks!) to add to the bag where we kept our gold which we would take into the assay office, have weighed and cashed in.

It was my understanding that the old prospectors used panning a lot to determine a good place to "stake a claim." Panning for them was a quick way to determine if there was any gold in a likely looking place and if it looked promising, they would then stake a claim. I remember seeing depictions of old prospectors and their burros with a gold pan and a pick hanging on the burro's back. If the panning indicated that the place was promising enough then you dug. I never heard of anyone "striking it rich" just by panning.

Sometimes Mother and I panned together and sometimes I panned alone, with Daddy and Vance keeping an eye on me. It was hard, tedious work and I would get tired and bored after a while and go on to something else. Daddy and Vance led the "real" operation with their Model A motor, water hose, water pump and sluice box. What they were doing was "big" and I always tried to be on hand when they collected the gold dust and

---

[20] Remember, any inaccuracies are those formed in the mind of a five-year-old although my parents did believe I could understand anything I was curious about and usually taught me along the way when anything of interest came up.

"nuggets" from the scraps of carpet at the bottom of the sluice box. That was the exciting part. We kept some of the "nuggets" (they weren't very big, not like the big hunks you read about in the papers) in a little glass vial to show the folks back home.

What Daddy and Vance set up for gold mining was quite impressive.

*Things were going good. We spent time building up the sluice box and getting the motor and the pump all mounted on a skid because we had planned to test it out there by the camp. After we got it running, we were going to get a cable across the river and swing it across the river and drag it about a mile up the canyon, up Clear Creek.* [21] *There was a spot up there Vance had sort of staked out. It had good promise. We got set up there by the camp, ran the equipment, saw how it worked, and got all the bugs out of it. We were making expenses plus some. And about that time, Germany started kicking up. I think they had invaded Belgium and a few other places and we felt we better sit still and see what takes place.*

## The Trips to Town

*Inasmuch as we were paying expenses and maybe a little more – maybe not – we went into Yreka once every ten days, because Manilla could never buy enough groceries to last a full month.* [22] *And going into town, Vance always had to have one of those great enormous candy bars which you don't see anymore. That was his touch with civilization.*

What my dad didn't seem to remember was that I always got one of these big chocolate bars too. I really looked forward to those candy bars.

---

[21] Can you imagine this? Wasn't the road enough?!

[22] He may mean here that we didn't have enough cash to buy a full month's groceries because we always cashed in our gold when we went in. Or, it may be because my mother liked her fresh vegetables – especially, young dandelion, dock, polk, lambs quarter, and plankton which she gathered from the fields and forests in the Ozarks to augment our diet and she did not know or find the same bounty in California.

I didn't think it was my "touch with civilization." I didn't particularly want to be in touch with civilization. Nothing could be better than our camp. And, I sure liked those candy bars. They were Hershey's milk chocolate – sometimes, they had nuts in them. I preferred the ones with nuts. Being a Southerner, I believed that there should be nuts in everything. As best I can remember they were about ten inches long, four inches wide, and about an inch thick. Boy, were they thick. Of course, I didn't have a firm grasp on inches at that time, though my parents had been teaching me, and that's about the size I figure it now. For sure, it wasn't one of those puny little candy bars. These bars were big! I could feel my eyes sparkling and my tummy just dancing as I stood at the counter looking at them and waiting my turn. Vance always ate his right away. I never could understand that. I saved mine and had a little bit each day. I only ate my last bite when I knew we were going to town the next day. Some days I was too busy and forgot, so I just had more for another day. Some days I gave Vance a piece if he looked like he needed it. I believe those big bars cost a nickel apiece. That was a lot of money then.

> We bought our gasoline and emergency supplies in Happy Camp, but we could save money by going on into Yreka and buying a big gob of groceries.
>
> Anyway, when we went into buy groceries, there was a section of road, we called it the ups and downs, because it went up-down, up-down, just like a wave. I didn't know it until some time later – I knew Vance said, "Oh, don't hit these roads so hard." I just thought, you know, backseat driver. But Elizabeth Anne got a kick out of it and so did I. We'd hit those and go flying and go down and up again and down again – and up again. [23] Just after these ups and downs was this spring. [24] And Vance had to stop at that spring and rest a while and get a drink of water. The problem was with these ups and downs, the way I was

---

[23] It was like a mini roller coaster and not scary. My uncle Leslie and I used to call them "dumps" back home. This was Daddy's version of careless driving – to speed up and go over these things. It always got a squeal out of Mother and me, which I think he liked.

[24] I believe the spring was after the ups and downs on the way home from town, not the way to town.

*driving, was making him sick. He didn't like to admit it*
*because he was a husky, wiry guy. If you ever saw a man*
*that was outstanding in stature, I think Vance was it.*

We all teased Vance a bit when we discovered that he was carsick. We
always teased each other all the time. That's the Indian way.

## Life in Camp

After a short while we settled down into life in camp. I felt very safe
there. Lincoln, Silver and I had almost complete freedom and could go
pretty much wherever we wanted – within limits. (It was sort of like Watts!)
We could do whatever we wanted around camp except go near the river.
We could go up to the flat place where the car and trailer were parked, or
on up to Mr. Beck's. It was pretty much okay to go wherever we wanted on
the flat place, the orchard, and Mr. Beck's clearing. That was a lot. There
were all kinds of grasshoppers and bugs at the flat place and Mr. Beck's
clearing. I was always careful not to hurt the bugs or grasshoppers when I
caught them. The grasshoppers got "tobacco juice" on me once-in-a-while.
Sometimes I would put them in a jar with holes in the lid that Mother had
fixed for me and I would always turn them loose again. That was important.
They had their lives, too. Then I had the trail up and down from Mr. Beck's
camp to explore. There were a million things to look at there. Rocks, quartz
and granite, all different colors and types. My whole family liked rocks, so
I would pick them up and put them in my pocket (I always had pockets –
in everything – I needed them) and take them back to camp to show my
parents and add them to the rock collections we had in camp. Sometimes
I would see a plant I hadn't seen before and didn't know. I would try to
remember it carefully so I could describe it and tell Mother so we could
look it up in a book she bought which described plants of California. If
we couldn't find it in the book or I couldn't describe it well, Mother and I
would go back with the book to see if we could find out what it was. Mother
and I enjoyed that. She always liked to know everything she could about
the plants, animals, insects, and the birds. I also watched for birds on the
trail so I could get to know them.

From the camp, I could go the other direction – down to the sluice box.
Sometimes Mother even asked me to take a pail of food and some coffee
down to "the boys." That was fun. They would turn off the motor and take
a break and we would all have snacks. I, of course, never drank any coffee.

The cold water from the stream was great for me. Sometimes I would stay for a while to pan gold, pick up rocks, take off my cowboy boots and wade in the water or just hang around and watch the gold mining. It was on one of those visits to the sluice box that I did a terrible thing:

## The First Emergency/Responsibility

*And one night after everybody gets settled in bed, Vance was in bed, Manilla was in bed, I was in bed. I was asleep, Manilla was asleep, Vance was snoring. Elizabeth Anne wakes me up and says, "I left Silver down at the mine."*

*I says, "He'll be all right. He'll be there in the morning."*

*"Oh no, the bear will get him or something will eat him up."*

*So I dressed, well, I put my shoes on anyway,* [25] *take the flashlight and go down and get Silver and bring him back. These are the problems you run into with a girl that has a stick horse and honors that she is responsible for it.*

Daddy didn't realize how serious this situation was. I had been irresponsible. Silver was not only my main form of transportation, he was my horse to take care of and I had let him down. I had been so busy with what I was doing that I had forgotten him and had run off without him. That was not acceptable to me. Mother had taught me that animals are a gift given to us – just like Silver had been. It is our responsibility to take care of them. Since they're "ours," they can't fend for themselves. We always fed the stock and the chickens, when we had them, before we ate. I could not be expected to sleep while Silver was out in the dark and cold by himself. And, since it was dark and late, Daddy had to help me out with this one. I was very grateful that he was willing to do it this one time. I never left Silver at night again.

As I said, I had my territory pretty well staked out and, frankly, it was about as big an area as I could take care of anyway. There were some simple things that were expected of me. I had to let Mother know when I was going to the sluice box and I had to let Daddy or Vance (Daddy was best) know when I went back to camp. I had to let Mother or whoever was in camp

---

[25] Daddy always slept in his shorts and undershirt.

know when I was going to go up to the flat place or Mr. Beck's house and I had to let Mr. Beck know when I was going back to camp. I couldn't go near the river without a grownup (Silver and Lincoln didn't count as grown ups. They were about my age, I figured, in matters like this.) And, I shouldn't get too far off the trails in the woods. I could go in only so far to still be able to see the trail. Other than that and caring for Silver and Lincoln, I had no real responsibilities and life was pretty free and easy. I often helped Mother out or Daddy or Vance or Mr. Beck, but that seemed kind of "voluntary."

## Sluice Box

Perhaps I need to say something about the sluice box and how the mining operation worked – from my memory, of course. I remember the sluice box as being a long, narrow, wooden thing – probably eight to ten feet or more long. Daddy has already described how he and Vance bent the metal so that it would catch what they wanted and let the rest go on down. Frankly, I didn't know much about that part. I just saw them working at it. They set up the sluice box on the bank so that it tilted down toward the river from top to bottom and the water would just naturally run downhill. They used the water pump to send a powerful stream of water to wash dirt, sand, rocks and whatever, sending these careening down the sluice box. The Model A motor was used to power the water pump – I believe. I'm not sure of that. The water pump may have had its own power supply. If so it would have had to be gasoline (no electricity out there). I don't think it did, however, and believe it was run off the engine. As the debris fed down the sluice box with some force behind it, most of the dirt and debris went on down and was deposited at the bottom. The gold and gold dust, however, in the process, because they were heavier, would fall to the bottom and be caught by the scraps of carpet Daddy and Vance had placed there. We would collect the gold "nuggets" and gold dust by cleaning off and shaking out the scraps of carpet. That was the most exciting time of the day. It was like a treasure hunt always with the hope that we would find a big one and "strike it rich." That never happened and that was okay too. We had enough and it was great fun. Not that Daddy and Vance didn't work hard. They did. They were literally "mining for gold." Instead of digging a hole in the ground and hacking away with picks and shovels, they were washing loose dirt that had picked up or held gold and "mining" the gold out of that with water. Just holding the fire hose with that powerful stream was hard work. They were always sweaty, wet, and filthy after a day's work. Some days were worse than others because the equipment broke down or they had to move or repair the sluice box. They would come back to the camp wet, tired and hungry. They usually felt better after they had bathed, (Mother and I always had hot water ready) shaved, and eaten. Often, they just fell into bed exhausted right after supper. Mother and I would try to keep quiet so as not to disturb them – not that I think anything could. And, there was always the sound of the trees and the river. Even though the work was hard, they seemed to love it. They talked, joked, teased, and horsed around. They did have something that was theirs to show for a day's work and "their time was their own," as they said. Whenever they needed a break, we took one – a trip to town, a special outing, friends over for dinner and an evening around the campfire. There was always a lot to do.

## Mother's Cooking

One of the best things about life on the Klamath River was Mother's cooking. She had a white gas camp stove and a campfire and that was it. We had gasoline lanterns hung over the table from the frame that held up the tarps and flashlights plus the campfire for light. I don't remember having any coolers and I'm sure that my dad rigged up something with the water from the river or the stream to keep things cool. He always did that kind of thing. We had to hang bacon, meat and other similar "interesting" items like that from the trees or keep it in a tight box so as not to attract bears, skunks, raccoons and other such animals. All food had to be put away at night. All the dishes were washed in a dishpan with hot water heated on the stove. Then, we always had a big pan of hot water that we dipped the dishes in to rinse off the soap and clean them before we dried them. Even I knew never, never to use soap on the good, black, cast-iron skillets, the spiders, and the big cast-iron Dutch oven. You just wiped them out or if necessary used some hot water to clean up "stuck places" but you simply didn't use soap. Soap would ruin the seasoning and they would have to be seasoned again, which was a lot of work. We always wiped them with oil inside and out before we put them away. The big black skillets and the Dutch oven were our most prized and valued cooking utensils. We took very good care of them. Mother and I usually did the clean up together – unless I was too tired, like at night. It was fun. We talked about our days and what we had done and discovered. Sometimes Mother recited poems or we sang songs while we worked. I loved the song *Patona*, which was a story about a very beautiful and very brave horse in New Mexico when the "West was won." I loved it when she would sing that and I would work very hard at clean up.

In the morning, Mother would get up before any of the rest of us would roll out of our warm beds. As Daddy said, the sun never reached us until mid-morning so Mother would light a lantern and the campfire. We always made sure we had plenty of wood and kindling for the fire before we went to bed. Daddy and Vance helped with wood gathering, although Mother and I did a lot of it ourselves. The rest of us usually got up when we smelled the bacon and the coffee. Mother always made a big, hot breakfast to "send the men off with a good start." Now, don't get me wrong here. Mother was not really a "housewife" type. There's nothing wrong with that, she just wasn't it. She was first and foremost a poet, writer, horsewoman and artist. She liked the "creative" aspects of housekeeping – like cooking, sewing, and decorating and being outdoors with animals and such and hated and basically ignored cleaning and "keeping house." We always said that Mother wouldn't even think to wash the kitchen floor until your feet stuck to it (a bit of an exaggeration but you get the point). So, even though she cooked up a storm at the camp, this did not mean that the majority of her time was spent cooking and cleaning and taking care of the men. She had her own life in camp – sewing, writing letters to Grandma Reed and the Willey's and others, walking, thinking and planning. She was as busy as the rest of us.

As I said, the smells of breakfast usually got the three of us out of bed. Mother always varied the meals so they were interesting. My favorite breakfast, I think, (they were all good) was when she fried up (actually it was more like poached because she didn't use fat and the ham made its own juices) big pieces of home-cured ham (We used a lot of cured meats for obvious reasons.) When we bought fresh meats, we would have one or two days of the fresh-cooked meats and she would then have to cook the rest up so it would keep longer. She would then reheat it. We also had canned meats. Back to the ham – she would cook thick pieces of a ham slice or two in the frying pan. In the meantime in the Dutch oven, she would be cooking homemade biscuits she had thrown together. When the ham was cooked, she would put it on a tin plate (you know one of those blue and white enameled plates – that's what we ate off of) and put the plate with the ham on it on the back of the cast-iron "griddle" over the campfire. The coffee would be perking away at the same place. While we all washed up, she opened a can of condensed cream or milk and then slowly poured this into the skillet where the ham had been fried. The skillet was sweet and salty with the juices of the ham and as she was pouring in the cream, she was scraping the bottom of the pan to loosen all the crispy little bits of ham and dried juices that had stuck to it. Just about then we would be washed, ready to eat and rushing to the table, the biscuits in the Dutch oven would be done, and the ham was warm and waiting. We would sit down and have a feast, an absolute feast. Daddy always said that the ham-cream gravy over biscuits with ham and steaming hot coffee was a feast fit for a king and he and Vance ate like two hungry kings.

Some mornings we had bacon, eggs and fried potatoes with onions in them. Mother always liked to add a little green chili if she had it. Mother liked Mexican food so hot it cleaned out your nose and head. Daddy didn't like food too hot so she was careful and put extra spices on the side for "those who liked it" – mostly herself.

Then, there were pecan pancakes with maple syrup made with the pecans we had brought from Arkansas with either eggs or bacon on the side. Another favorite was a big pot of oatmeal with apples (usually Mr. Beck had given those to us) and cinnamon and eggs on the side. Eggs kept well, were cheap, and, I now realize, added protein. Mother believed in good balanced meals and always tried to have juice or fruit on hand for breakfast – mostly canned, of course, because canned things kept. Then, there was canned corned beef hash, a whole big skillet full with eggs broken into little holes made in it, looking out like glazed eyes when she put it on the table. She would heat up the corned beef, turning and turning it in the skillet, then she would turn down the fire on the camp stove a bit, make little dents in it and break the eggs into the dents – two or three each for "the boys" and one each for us. Then she would put the skillet back on the fire with the lid from the Dutch oven over it and the eggs would cook. She said that this way of cooking eggs was somewhere between poaching and coddling them. They sure were good. She usually served that with toast, toasted over the campfire on the cast-iron plate – with butter, homemade apple butter and jam, or honey if you wanted it plus some fruit and coffee, of course, for the grownups. Sometimes, if the morning was chilly or at night when there was a chill in the air, she would make me some "teakettle tea" to drink with the grownups. That was really a special treat – hot water from the teakettle poured over milk and honey or sugar – it was usually condensed milk, of course.

And that was only breakfast! We ate like horses but I didn't think one of us ever gained an ounce. We worked it off as soon as we ate it.

"We were just working too hard to gain any weight," Mother said. "We needed to be fed well." Of course, old Lincoln who had been guarding the car all night and working hard during the day, had already been fed by the time we sat down to breakfast. Silver, on the other hand, didn't eat much and I also let him graze in the clearing while I did things with Mr. Beck.

Lunches were usually a hot, homemade soup and some kind of sandwiches. If Mother had any access to any kind of greens at all she would make a big salad. She loved salads. If there was nothing "fresh" to work with, she would mix up canned grapefruit and/or orange sections with some coconut and oil and vinegar or some canned peas with chopped up onions and cheese bits mixed with mayonnaise. She was very creative and could make a great meal out of almost nothing. Nothing was ever wasted. That was our way. We used every bit of everything. If we had a whole ham, we would bake it and eat off the whole ham, then she would have ham steaks, then she would use little bits for seasoning with greens, green beans or eggs or soup. She would boil up the bone and make a several day soup with black-eyed peas, beans, onions, carrots or whatever. She would render the fat out of the skin and make cracklings to be used in biscuits or for snacks and the fat she got out of the rendering would be used for frying, for seasoning and for a "special treat" on Lincoln's food. She said it was never right to waste food and we didn't.

Dinners were the best time of all and always made the ending of every day special. On rainy or "grey" days, Mother often would have a big stew cooking all day over the campfire. She would never do this on the camp stove because gasoline was expensive and hard to come by. Since fires had to be tended and watched, she would usually stay around the camp on those days. Sometimes she would cook a pot roast with lots of potatoes, onions, rutabagas, and carrots cooked with it. Usually, she made a gravy with the pot roast. Sometimes, we just had a big macaroni and cheese with vegetables on the side. Whatever she cooked, it was always good! I think she liked being appreciated and appreciation was not in short supply. It didn't take long for word to get out that there was good food at our place and fairly regularly one of the bachelors, widowers or other miners used to drop by just before dinner time, always bringing something with them, usually store bought, like cookies or something grown like apples. Whatever it was, Mother could use it. She always invited them to stay. They would hem and haw and then accept. She would always say something like "You're going to stay for dinner, aren't you? We can always add another cup of water to the soup." That would break the tension and they would always stay. They said they came to see Daddy and Vance and see how the mining was going but I always suspected that they were coming because of Mother's cooking. No matter, it gave us a break and it was fun. Of course, their arrival usually meant a night around the campfire talking – about something – almost anything. Everyone would pitch in with clean up and then we would all gather around the fire for an evening of storytelling and visiting. At some point, Mother would slip away unnoticed and whip up something special, throw it into the Dutch oven and quietly set it over the fire. We knew she had done it again when we began to smell it. No matter how I tried, I never could keep my mouth from watering as those smells drifted over the camp. When they blended with the sway of the trees, the roar of the river, and the hum of the grownups talking, I couldn't imagine that the heaven that the preacher back in the Ozarks had talked about could be any better than this. Just when I would start to doze off leaning against Daddy or old Lincoln, Mother would unveil our "treat" – pineapple upside-down cake dumped out on a platter with rings of pineapple and brown sugar and pineapple juice glaze streaming down the sides of a white cake, or brownies, apple cobbler, blackberry pie, apple Brown Betty with cinnamon and sparkling grains of sugar on the top, or walnut cake with caramel glaze. We never ceased to be amazed with what came out of that Dutch oven. Perhaps it was all that fresh air, the wood smoke, the nights, the tiredness of our bodies, or just all of our being and working together – I don't know. All I know is that the food we ate there in our camp is probably the best food I have ever tasted in my life and that includes the Queen Elizabeth II and some of the best restaurants in the world.

Cooking and eating wasn't all we did in camp and it did take up a fair amount of time. Mother and I gathered a lot of the firewood and Daddy and Vance pulled in the big stuff and took an axe to it. We had a small hatchet that Mother used to chop limbs and small trees and I could use when Mother watched. Mother and I both liked being in the woods so gathering wood was fun.

## Mr. Beck

At least once a day we took up something to Mr. Beck. He was, after all, an elder and that's what you did with elders. Whenever we made anything, we always put a dish aside for Mr. Beck. Sometimes Lincoln, Silver and I took it up and sometimes Mother went with us. Often, I went up to see Mr. Beck and stayed around his place in the afternoons. Mother liked to take naps in the afternoon. I didn't. I could play at camp when she napped and I had to be quiet – not that I was that noisy. I always talked to Lincoln, Silver, and my toys quietly but we had a rule in our family – sleep was like, well, sleep was like church – it was sort of holy. When anyone was sleeping, everyone else kept quiet. That's just the way it was. Mother called it respect. She used that word a lot. Anyway, when she napped, I usually went to Mr. Beck's or down to the sluice box. Mr. Beck was usually my first choice.

I have already described Mr. Beck and what he looked like when I first saw him. He never looked much different the whole time we were there. He changed shirts now and again and I supposed he changed pants. If he did, they all looked pretty much the same. One day I asked him why he always wore long underwear (I could see it) even in the summer.

"Well, Elizabeth Anne, I don't know. I guess it's just because I'm used to wearing 'em. You could always catch a chill, you know."

I reckoned he was right about that. He told my mother one day that I asked some purty good questions. I guess I did. I just wanted to know a lot of things, it seemed.

Mother was always concerned that I would be a bother to Mr. Beck. She would always say, "Now don't you be a bother to Mr. Beck." I didn't want to be a bother to him either and I didn't know any way to find out if I was being a bother to him except to ask.

So, I asked, "Mr. Beck, am I being a bother to you? Mother doesn't want me to be a bother to you."

"Gracious, no, Elizabeth Anne, you're no bother," he said.

So I took it that I was no bother. And when Mother would say that I might be a bother, I would tell her, "I'm no bother, Mother. Mr. Beck says so." Nevertheless, every once-in-awhile it seemed that she had to check it out for herself and would go up to ask him. (I never took it personally that she did this. I just guessed it was something she needed to be really sure of. Of course I always told the truth. She knew that. "Don't ever lie, Elizabeth Anne. If I ever catch you in a lie, you'll get in a heck of a lot more trouble than if you'd told the truth." I took her at her word and figured it was much too much trouble to lie anyway.)

"I hope Elizabeth Anne's not too much trouble for you, Mr. Beck," Mother would say. "Goodness gracious, no," he would say, "she's a big help to me." I knew that. I think he liked my company.

I said before that when I first saw Mr. Beck after that awful first drive down that terrible road (Mother and I never quite got used to it. I did better than she did, I think), that he looked kindly and I figured that he and I would be friends. I liked elders and had been around a lot of them up to that point in my life. Well, he sure proved me right early on. When we first unpacked Silver and I started riding him around (Silver needed to stretch his legs after having been cooped up for so long), Mr. Beck said, "That's a mighty fine horse you've got there."

"He sure is," I answered back.

"What's his name?" he asked.

"Silver," I said and then yelled out a, "Hi Ho Silver away" and took off. He chuckled and our friendship was cemented.

According to Daddy:

> Beck had come in that country in the gold rush days and brought the first packload of food into the miners. I do not know what H.E. Beck's real last name was. I may have at one time. He may have told me, but he was a step-child. His step-father must have been pretty mean to him. When he was about 15 years old, he took off on his own. And I think he was about 16 or 17 when he brought the first mule train, pack train into the miners over the mountains. I imagine it was burros, he didn't say, he just called it a pack train but I believe it was burros or horses. [26] It was a pack train full of groceries and supplies and so on. That was real gold mining in those days. Gold was everywhere.
>
> Anyhow, Beck built his cabin, well I can't call it a cabin. It was quite a house. He married an Indian woman and had two boys, I believe. They worked for the Forest Service and I don't think he saw much of them.

I described the outside of Mr. Beck's house for you before. It was so solid and beautiful. I loved that great big porch wrapping around it supported by those big tree trunks. In the South, we would have called it a veranda and it would have been fancier and painted. But this was California and it seemed to fit in quite well just the way it was.

The inside of the house was dark as log houses tend to be and it smelled of living. I always notice the smell of things and it smelled of living. It was a

---

[26] My guess is it was most likely mules or burros – definitely not horses. Mules are much more sure-footed than horses and better for something like that. My dad never was much of a horseman. He left that to Mother and me.

good smell – a little musty, but not much. It smelled like a lot of bodies had lived there and now the smell was mostly Mr. Beck. Yet, I thought I could smell ghosts of other bodies there, too. There were also smells of cooking – lots of cooking with onions. I learn a lot by smelling. Sometimes there are things you learn by smelling that you can't learn any other way. The house also had a tinge of a smell of loneliness and tiredness – not much, just a little. I had expected it to be all musty and dusty and it wasn't. Oh, it wasn't spotless or fresh-smelling like those ads in magazines and the on radio or something – not like that. And it was dusted and comfortable. The couch and the chairs were a brown color and sagged a bit with a kind of weariness but they were comfortable. Actually, I liked that they sagged a bit because my feet could touch the floor. The kitchen was in the back and caught the morning sun. It had been partitioned off from the main room through a big open doorway. The right side of the living room looked south over the orchard and toward the river. The front looked west toward the berry patch where there were raspberries and blackberries across the little road that came in. Behind them were the grape arbor and more fruit trees. These were old fruit trees. Mr. Beck had been here a long time.

I think I spent more time with Mr. Beck than anybody else. Sometimes we talked a lot and sometimes we were just quiet. Like, for example, when we picked berries, we were usually quiet. He would say, "Well, Elizabeth Anne, how would you like to go pick some berries?" I think he knew because my eyes always turned into a sparkle and I could feel a huge grin creep across my face. I think now I would call it a rhetorical question. Then, even though I thought he knew, I would answer to be polite.

"Oh, I would love that, Mr. Beck." He would get up off the rocker on the porch and say, "You wait here. We'll need something to put them in." and off he would go with his somewhat rocking gait on those bowed legs. In no time, he would return with a gallon bucket in each hand. They looked big to me. Then, we would go down the steps. I kinda looked out for him going down those steps because he seemed so old but I don't think he needed me. I think he was looking out for me. Anyway, we would walk over to the bushes and he would always say, "Now you can eat as many as you want but make sure you have some to take back to your family." The syrup buckets were great for berry picking because they had wire handles that would let them swing back and forth and they were easy to hold on to. Then silently we would start picking. I always liked picking the raspberries better than the blackberries because the thorns were not so mean and they didn't hook into your skin like the blackberries did. Mother always said it was better to wear long sleeves and long pants when picking blackberries. I wasn't always prepared but I was always game to give it a try. Of course, I did like both blackberries and raspberries and always took him at his word that I could eat some. I don't think I ate that many but he must have picked much faster than I did because he always had a very full bucket when mine was about half full.

"That should do it," he said. "Let's go up to the house and have a treat and something cool to drink."

"But I haven't finished mine," I said.

"That's all right. I'll give you my full one and I'll take your half one. The full one should be plenty for your family and the half one should be just about right for me to have all the berries I need."

That's the way he was. He was really nice that way.

So, we go back to his house and he sets out two big glasses of cold water on the table, and goes to the kitchen and brings out the big piece of pineapple upside-down cake we had given him yesterday and two plates and forks. I wasn't sure I should eat <u>his</u> cake. I had had mine the day before at our camp. He started to cut it in two and I said, "No, no, Mr. Beck. That's way too much. I'm not very hungry." I really didn't know what to do. I had just told him a bit of a fib. I could have eaten that whole piece and another one to boot but he <u>was</u> an elder and I knew he really liked these treats we sent up and, after all, he was an elder. I think Mother would say that was all right that I told a little fib under the circumstances – I really didn't want to eat his cake. So we sat down to have our water and cake. We sure enjoyed that treat break. Then, I said, "Well, thank you, Mr. Beck for the cake and the water <u>and</u> the berries. I better get these berries down to Mother. She might want to use them for supper."

"Get along, then," he said. Secretly I was thinking that one of us would probably be bringing him up some blackberry cobbler tonight or in the morning.

Mr. Beck was really generous. He had quite a few apple trees and he told me to "feel free just to take any I found on the ground." Well, I took him seriously, and sometimes this was quite a few. I never picked any but I kept the ground pretty clean. Sometimes I would have to make two or three trips with the skirt of my dress full or get Mother to help after I had piled them up. We had stewed apples, apple sauce, apples baked with cinnamon, sugar and nuts in the Dutch oven, apple-celery-walnut salad (I believe Mother called it Waldorf salad, I didn't know why), apple pancakes or just eating apples. We ate a lot of apples that summer. Then he gave us some grapes and peaches, too. He really was generous. He gave us lots from his garden, too – carrots (grated carrot-raisin salad and stews), squash, tomatoes, and corn. Oh, how I loved that corn. It made me think of the Ozarks more than anything else. I was never homesick. Home was wherever my family was. And I did like both places – the Ozarks and California. Right then, I sure was having a great time on the Klamath River.

One of the things I liked most was when he let me help him work in the garden. He'd say, "Oh, good. I'm glad to see that you have your cowboy hat on today. How would you like to help me work in the garden?"

"I'd like that," I said.

"Great! Let me get my hat and we'll see how much damage we can do in the garden today," he'd say as he headed for the door with me right behind him. We'd go through the cool darkness of the house, he'd grab whatever he needed, and we'd head out the back door to the garden. He always said that was one of the good things about a log house – they were cool in summer and warm in the winter (with a fire in the stove!).

He had a huge garden just filled with healthy plants. He told me that his wife had taken care of it when she was alive but since she had died it had fallen to him to do it if he wanted fresh vegetables and he really liked those fresh vegetables. I reckon that it saved him money, too, just like what he gave us saved us money. He always said that he was glad to have such a fine young helper now in his old age. He knew I liked to hear that. There were times that he was a bit stiff and had a hard time bending over and then I would do the bending for him. That was easy for me and that's what you do with elders. I used to do that for Grandma Reed, too. It seemed pretty easy for me to bend over and, after all, I was closer to the ground anyway.

Some days we would just pick vegetables. The peas and beans were the most fun because they climbed, were up on sticks called trestles and you had to hunt for them in the leaves. It seemed like the more you picked the more there were. They just kept producing. Sometimes pulling the carrots was hard because they were so big and the ground would be hard if we hadn't hoed or if it hadn't rained. We had to hoe and pull weeds quite a bit. He had an old hoe with a broken handle that was just about my size so we each had one. He told Daddy that he sure got a lot of work out of me. I think my parents were glad that I could help Mr. Beck out. He was letting us stay on his land and everything.

The most interesting part of gardening with Mr. Beck was when we went after the bugs. He was not about to let those bugs take over his garden. He didn't spray or anything like that. It was like he knew every plant and what it needed. One day he decided we "needed to take care of the potato plants" as he put it. He put a little kerosene in a tin can and we headed for the garden. His potatoes were flowering and the potato beetles had discovered them. He picked one off and showed me.

"These are bad bugs. They'll ruin the potatoes," he said as he dropped them in the can of kerosene. Now Mother had said that there's no such thing as a bad bug or anything in nature for that matter. (She wasn't so sure about people sometimes.) But, these were Mr. Beck's potatoes and he'd need them that winter so I thought I better help him out. Now he had a completely different attitude toward the tomato worms, those big juicy green ones. We put them in a can, too, but there was no kerosene in it. He had me take them down to the apple orchard and dump them "so the birds could eat them," saying maybe they'd leave the apples alone if they had some fat, juicy worms all laid out for them. I asked him why he didn't do that with the potato beetles and he said they'd just come right back and besides he didn't think they tasted too good because we had never seen the birds after them in the garden. I guess he knew what he was talking about. I liked working in the garden with Mr. Beck and, believe you me, I never went home empty handed.

The other thing Mr. Beck and I would do was sit on the porch and rock and talk. That old man would talk to me just like I was somebody. Sometimes both of us were just too tired (or lazy!) to work so we would just sit and wile the hours away while he reminisced and remembered when he was young. He would tell wonderful stories. The great thing about elders is that they have time. Parents are often too busy with all the things they have to do. Elders seem to have the time just to sit and talk and remember. Kids have that kind of time, too. It's a good thing to get kids and elders together, I think.

One day, he talked about "the old days."

"You know, Elizabeth Anne, this country ain't what it used to be." (He had used the word ain't. Now Mother had told me never to use that word. It was something like "nigger" I guess – well maybe a little. We weren't supposed to use that word either. She said "nigger" would offend and wasn't nice. It wasn't that "ain't" wasn't nice. It just wasn't a proper word. She said that people would think we weren't educated and didn't know how to talk right if we used ain't. Well, Mr. Beck was educated – he sure knew a lot, anyway – and he was ninety-two years old so I figured he could use any words he wanted at that stage.) He'd say something like that and then wait a while. It gave me a lot of time to think. I guess he thought, too. Sometimes, it seemed like he just drifted off for a while. Not sleep, mind you, he wasn't one of those old people who would fall asleep all the time. No sir, I never saw him fall asleep when we were sitting talking. He did say that he was "going to go take a rest now" like after we had worked in the garden. But, he knew he was doing it and went and took a rest. His drifting off wasn't like he was falling asleep. It was like he had gone back to gather some memories and bring them back all ready to dump on the porch and sort them through. I didn't mind waiting and was eager to see what he had brought back.

"Nope," he said. "It ain't the same." (See, he went right back to what he was talking about.) "When I first came to this country, it was mostly Indians. There were very few white people and they were prospectors and miners – they were a pretty rowdy bunch, a bunch of hooligans. Most were not men you could trust or would want to turn your back on. There was the odd one could be trusted but you never really knew which one that was until you'd knowed him for a long time. So I didn't spend much time finding out. I made friends with the Indians. They sure knew this country, those Indians did. They knew every inch of it. It was their land after all. The white people just moved right in on them. Took their land. Those white people wouldn't've been interested if some darn fool hadn't discovered gold. Guess I can't complain – got me in here, didn't it? This here land was the most beautiful place I had ever seen. The Indians had taken real good care of it. It wasn't messed up at all until the white fellas came." Then he'd stop for a while. That was kinda what Mother had told me, too – about the Indians.

Then he'd start in again.

"Take this piece of land here. When I got it, there was nothing here. I – me and my mules – cleared this place here. It was all forest like down where you're staying. All those trees in this house came off this land. Took me a long time to clear this land – lot of hard work. I skidded those logs with my mules. My wife was an Indian woman. Sometimes the Indians helped me."

It was hard for me to imagine this big yard, garden, orchard and clearing all as woods and I believed him.

Mr. Beck and I spent many times like that on his porch. He'd remember funny little things like the time he was skidding a log with his mules and a mountain lion showed up and those mules went crazy. They were dragging Mr. Beck all over the place. Or the time that one of the miners got drunk and fell in the river and drowned. "Never found him," Mr. Beck said matter-of-factly. Some thought it might not have been an accident as "his claim had just come in." (That means he had found gold.) Mr. Beck said that it was not a good idea to let others know your claim had come in or you might have an "accident" like that. In a mining camp, it was best to keep your "mouth shut and your eyes down." That's why Mr. Beck hung out with the Indians I guess.

Then a terrible thing happened to Mr. Beck. Daddy tells it better than I do. I just remember I rode to town on Mother's lap with Mr. Beck stretched out in the back seat. He sure was sick. I was afraid he was going to die. Vance, Lincoln, and Silver stayed back at camp 'cause we didn't have enough room in the '36 Chevy.

Here's how Daddy remembered it.

> One morning, I get up, sun was up, it was hot. I go up to the car to get something, I look up toward Beck's house. Here he is standing out in the sun. He has a big coat on, he is all wrapped up. His arms all held together like he was freezing to death. I couldn't figure out what was going on there, so I take what I was going after, and go back down to camp. I mention it and Vance and I decide to go up and see what is wrong with the old man, because he was a nice old man. We go up there, and he is shaking like a . . . well, I won't say it, a dog and peach seeds is part of the story. I don't think you want that . . . you can't print it. He was really shaking. We asked him, "What's wrong Beck?"
>
> "Oh," he says. "I think I'm having a congested chill." I looked at Vance, I thought he knew. He looked at me, thought I knew. So we go down and get Manilla, does she know? No. But we better all go up and see what is wrong.
>
> "Put him to bed," she says. "Build up a fire." She put him to bed, and we cover him up. And the Forest Service at Happy Camp had an emergency people shack, office or whatever you want to call it and a registered nurse on duty. I think she was running it. So we give her a ring on the telephone. Yes, she would be right down. Of course it took her about, oh, 30 minutes to an hour to get there. And she says, "Well, you done all I know to do. I think we will have to take him into the hospital." She says, "I'll call the ambulance."
>
> Beck says, "I'm not riding in the ambulance until I'm dead." And he says, "They'll take me," pointing to Vance

and me and Manilla. So, ok. She called ahead to make arrangements for him, talked to the doctor and he didn't know what was wrong of course. It's hard to diagnose a person over the telephone.

Anyway, we load the old man in the car and take off and every once in a while we would hit a bump and he would groan. We got in there about eight o'clock. It was dark. Everybody had gone home. But the nurse had made all the arrangements, so we check him in – just a matter of turning him over to the nurse – not like it is now. And she asked him a few questions and rings the doctor. I don't know what all the conversation was, but I do remember her saying, "Yes, Doctor, he took a box of Ex-lax with excellent results." And pretty soon she says, "The doctor will be right in," and we all go into a little private room, you know, where they take the patients. The doctor comes in after a while and pulls Beck's shirt up and starts poking around on his belly. Boy, he was pushing hard, and Beck never did grunt or groan or anything. He was a tough, old guy. Well, somebody had taken a blood sample, and he came back in and the doctor says,

"Well how high was it?" asks the doctor.

"I don't remember the figures," the lab man says, "I didn't even finish counting them, I didn't finish the count."

So the doctor turned to us and says, "Are you relatives?"

We says, "No, just his friend. We brought him in."

"Well," he says. "You'll have to get out, we are going to operate right now. He's got an appendicitis."

And old Beck gave Manilla his billfold, his watch, and something else, probably a ring or something. We went out and asked the nurse – we had already sat there for an hour or so – and asked the nurse how long it would take for an appendicitis operation.

She says, "If everything goes right, about 20-30 minutes."

Well, we'd been there a long time, at least it seemed that way. And finally, after I had read all the magazines, all the newspapers, walked around the rooms and walked *around the lobby there and looked at all the stuff on the walls, and what was on the floor and all, and in the corners, finally, the doctor comes out and says, "The old man is doing fine. His appendix must have ruptured sometime yesterday. But he's ok, we've washed him all out, sewed him up, and we think he will be all right."*

*And so he says, "There is nothing more you folks can do, if you want to go home." So, we told him where home was.*

*"Well," he says. "We'll call you if anything goes wrong."*

*So we go to town. We hadn't had dinner. We hadn't had lunch in today's terms. We went to this restaurant, asked for a menu, and they give us a breakfast menu! When you miss two meals, you know, you don't want pancakes and syrup. Somewhat insulted, we asked if they didn't have something more substantial.*

*He says, "Folks, it's four o'clock in the morning!"*

*Well, we didn't know that. So we explained it to him.*

*So he says, "Here, I'll see what I can dig up."*

*We said, "Anything, we don't care, hot or cold." He really fixed us up a nice meal, a real good meal.*

*So after we've eaten, we take off to go down the Klamath River Road, 90 miles, and we was listening to the radio. There were two radio stations we could get out there. One was WWL in New Orleans and the other was KFI, I think it was, either Los Angeles or San Francisco. You are setting right down in a hole, and radio reception is not very good. But we had the radio on going on down the road, half asleep, half awake. All of a sudden, right across the front of the car, jumps a big, old mountain lion. Well, that startled us, woke us up. From then on we kept looking for things, and as usual, we didn't see any eyes or anything else all the way down there.*

*So we went on home, went to bed, slept a half a day, got up and started mining again.*

That old man had walked around for two days, been driven ninety miles over an impossible, bumpy dirt road, gone through emergency surgery and still survived. I'm still impressed with that. He must have had severe peritonitis. The doctor in that little hospital must have done a great job too. I had an emergency appendectomy in the 1980's in a thoroughly modern hospital and it was no piece of cake and I was nowhere near his age, nor as sick as he was!

Old Lincoln was so glad to see us (and the car!) back. I think he was pretty nervous while we were gone. Vance decided to stay up at Mr. Beck's house in case we got a phone call and had to rush back into the hospital. I was sure glad we were there when he got sick.

I missed him terribly. It seemed like he stayed in the hospital for a really long time. My parents kept saying things like "I hope he makes it," and "He's a tough old geezer." I didn't know much about praying. The preacher used to drone on for a long time in church and called it praying. Honestly, to me, sometimes it just sounded like a lot of noise and that he didn't know when to stop. I couldn't imagine that God was interested in all that carrying on and sometimes, I secretly believed that it was more for the preacher than for God so I tried to keep it simple.

"Please God, let Mr. Beck be okay." I didn't have much else to say really. (You'll of course remember, that my last and only other, as far as I can remember, serious attempt at praying was on the roller coaster and I didn't have a lot of time then!)

We made sure to take care of his garden and his house. Mother and Vance and I did that. (Daddy hadn't fallen into his love of gardens and weeding them yet. That came later in his life when he thought that I should have the same interest and made me weed. That wasn't like working in Mr. Beck's garden – work with Mr. Beck was fun.) Sometimes I would go up there and work alone – with Silver and Lincoln, of course. I wanted to make sure it looked just as good when he came back as it did when he left. I loved that old man.

It was necessary that I take charge of the tomato worms. Mother was deathly afraid of worms. She had no fear at all of snakes and she would faint if a worm got on her. If she even saw one in the house, she would scream and I would have to rescue her. She especially hated those inchworms. She said she couldn't stand the way they reared up and looked at you. I thought they were kinda cute. Anyway, I didn't even want to take a chance of Mother's passing out so I said I would take care of the tomatoes. It was better if she didn't go near them.

Finally, Mr. Beck came home. Since he wouldn't be lying down in the back seat, (They had kept him in the hospital awhile because his appendix had ruptured.) if I sat in Mother's lap, we all could go into pick him up, including Lincoln, which he was happy about. What a happy occasion that was. Mr. Beck was sure eager to get home. Daddy drove carefully and when we got there, you could tell Mr. Beck was tired but his eyes sure lit up when he saw his place – how good it looked. Vance stayed up at his place with him for a week or so to make sure he was all right and I checked in on him every morning and afternoon while Vance was working with Daddy. Mother made sure that he didn't have to bother about cooking and soon he seemed just about back to normal. I sure was relieved.

I think I didn't realize how much I loved Mr. Beck until I started writing this. Maybe he took my Great-Grandma Reed's place. She had certainly been the most important person in my life until age three and then very significant until she died. I knew Grandma and Grandpa Willey loved me and they didn't have much time for me. Grandma Reed and Mr. Beck had all the time in the world for me. Now, they didn't always stop what they were doing to talk to me. They just included me in what they were doing – and sometimes they just talked with me and did nothing else. They both also taught me all kinds of things and they both knew a lot about almost everything – plants, animals, the way people were and weren't – who to trust and who not to turn your back on – how times were when they were young and what their parents had taught them about what times were like when they were young. Who else could teach you things like that? They were always teaching me and seemed to just assume I could learn it. If I was confused, questions were just fine. They also talked to me like I was an equal – maybe not really an equal – they just seemed to assume that I could understand and would be interested. And I was! Perhaps Mr. Beck really had filled the vacuum left by my Grandma Reed. I don't know and I guess it doesn't really matter. This I know – Mr. Beck was Mr. Beck and he had and still holds a very important place in my life. Every child should have a Great-Grandma Reed and a Mr. Beck in her/his life. But it has to be someone really old to have that much time and patience. I really have enjoyed this long visit with him as I have been writing this book and it feels like that toe-headed, little five-year-old has taken over the "telling" completely.

## A Skunk in Camp

As I said, the sun always took its time getting to our camp. Although we were situated in a small clearing, this clear space was surrounded by towering trees that circled us with great majesty and protection. These trees protected us from things we didn't want, like intruders and such, and they also protected us from that which we did want, like the sun. In spite of this "protection" and the cool darkness that infused the camp until the sun was high in the sky, we always rose early. There was so much to do. One day we ate a hearty breakfast of oatmeal, bacon, pancakes and of course, coffee for the adults. Even the meals were fun – eating in a group like that with everyone joking and telling stories. I loved it. What a treat for a five-year-old to be in on all of this!

After breakfast, the men went off to the sluice box to "mine" for gold and Mother and I then had the day to ourselves with only lunch and dinner responsibilities. This day, by the time the breakfast clean up was done, the sun was filtering through the trees with rays of magic light spattering the clearing. I loved those rays! When those rays of rainbow light came filtering through and dispelling the morning mists, I was sure that they brought enchantment and magic with them. They played like visual music. The wood sounds and the river were their accompaniment as the trees swayed and groaned and crashed, creating new configurations of swaying light and adding dance and movement to the symphony being conducted in our little clearing. No laziness or temptation to stay in my warm bed could have seduced me. Every day's show, every day's symphony was different. I wanted to be there to participate and enjoy.

When the first rays arrived this day, Mother determined that it was the right day to do a wash. Her decision was also aided by the fact that "the men" and I had no clean clothes left. This was because the men and I did the really dirty work. They worked on the sluice box all day which was wet and dirty and I participated in almost everything that went on. Some days I worked on the sluice box too or I panned for gold in the stream near the sluice box, contributing my miniscule nuggets and gold dust to the pot to be taken to town and cashed in. I also helped gather wood and spent endless hours exploring the woods and trails – dirty work at best.

I helped Mother gather wood, build up the fire and do the wash. By the time we finished, it was time to take lunch to the men and we "picnicked" by the sluice box and stream. What a glorious time it was, full of stories and teasing. As Mother and I headed back to camp, the weather was beginning to change and the mists were starting to roll in. Mother had misjudged the weather. This miscalculating on the weather was very rare on her part. In fact, it almost never happened. I decided that it was because we were in California and not in Oklahoma where she was always right about the weather and knew what signs to read.

We rushed back to camp and took the still wet clothes off the line, which would have been in the sun if there had been any, and put them under the tarp canopy which made up our camp. My dancing beams of light were gone only to be replaced by drifting waves of mist which were equally beautiful and fascinating to watch. One could keep as busy watching them as the sun symphony.

Mother flew into action. I was dispatched to go into the woods and gather as much wood as I could before it got soggy – clearly an important task. I plunged in with gusto and dragged large, fallen limbs, small downed tree trunks, and all manner of treasures from the forest. We could chop them up with the axe later under the protective covering of the camp. We kept a roaring fire going all day hoping, to no avail, to dry the clothes. While we dried clothes (not too active a task after we had strung lines and draped them over every object available so that drying them meant an occasional turn for some) we busied ourselves cleaning up our camp. We put together a special hot meal of meat and vegetables with special herbs like bay leaves which we could gather there. Near camp we kept the meat and vegetables cooking on the campfire stove along with Dutch oven baked bread. I was excited to help prepare such a special meal and knew that the evening would be fun as we ate and talked. Mother even put me in my raincoat and sent me up to Mr. Beck's house to get some apples since she was going to make a Dutch oven apple cobbler this afternoon and I would take some up to him later. He waved me over and gave me a lemon drop to suck on the way back to camp with my sack of apples. Of course he would have some apple cobbler later.

What a glorious misty mystery day! By the time night was closing in and the men returned from the sluice box, I had delivered Mr. Beck's apple cobbler and helped with the meal. The smells were wonderful in our camp. Cinnamon, fresh-picked bay leaf, rosemary brought from Arkansas, meat, potatoes, carrots and, of course, apples. I just knew that every animal and person for miles wanted to be in our camp that night.

The men wanted to get out of their wet clothes but there was nothing dry to put on! The whole world felt soggy as we ate the feast Mother and I had prepared. Gratitude and praise flowed from the lips of the happy men and Mother and I shared a private glance and wink of a job well done.

They took off their wet shirts and wrapped themselves in blankets as we ate, and then came the hot apple cobbler with canned milk poured on it. What joy, what ecstasy. Mother (and I) had outdone herself (ourselves). Praises were unending and each mouthful was glorious. This was one night when the talk centered around the food and how great it was and the wonders of what can be done on a camp stove. Mother was, indeed, a genius, we all agreed and she was quick to remind everyone that the cobbler would not have been possible without Mr. Beck's apples and Elizabeth Anne's taking that long walk in the rain and picking them up and bringing them back. With both belly and heart full, I was happy to forego the usual stories around the fire and gratefully crawled, exhausted, into my dry bed which quickly warmed up with my body in it. Sleep came easily and I was out like a light.

Sometime later, I awoke with a commotion going on. I was so tired and warm I fell immediately back to sleep as it quieted down and only learned the full story of the happenings in the camp from my mother the next morning.

I guess my daddy had uncharacteristically gone to bed naked as he had no dry clothes to sleep in that night. He awoke to a disturbance in the camp. We usually packed everything away and hung edibles from ropes in the trees to keep the animals out of our food so were not too often troubled by scavengers in camp. This night was no different and I am sure those wonderful smells had made it different – at least for the animals.

Yet, for some time now, we had been having almost nightly visits from a friendly skunk. The skunk would knock over pots and pans, try to get in the food, scatter the garbage and generally make a nuisance of itself. We knew it was a skunk because it always left a "calling card" with a distinctive aroma. Some nights it was noisy and some nights not, yet, we always knew when it had been there.

According to my mother, that night along with the dampness, having no clothes, and really, really wanting a good night's sleep, my dad had had it. When the skunk began banging around in the camp and woke him up, Daddy had had enough! He tossed a bit and huffed and puffed as my mother told it and then jumped out of bed stark naked in a loud stage whisper so as not to wake me.

"I'm going to get that skunk once and for all."

Mother remembers mumbling something like, "Oh, Virgil," and rolling over. I slept through most of this. As she told me the story the next morning, she says she remembered thinking "the skunk can't get anything, let it go" and dozed off.

My dad burst out of the tent clothed only with his pistol to clear our camp of the dreaded skunk menace. By this point in the story, tears of laughter are rolling down my mother's face. He and his pistol took a brave, naked stance against the bothersome skunk. In a flash he was back in the tent with eyes wide and flashing. My dad was electric.

"It's a bear," he shouted to my mother. Slipping on his shoes, grabbing the 30/30 and bare as a jaybird he went after the bear. Luckily, the bear had lost interest and had ambled off into the woods, thwarting the bare hunter. By this point in her storytelling, my mother was convulsed in tears of laughter (and I was sorry I had slept through one of the most exciting nights in our camp and disappointed not at least to have seen the bear and I remember feeling a bit embarrassed about my father's nudeness as Mother told it. He was very modest and funny about those things so it was probably a good thing I didn't wake up.)

Here's my dad's version of the whole affair.

> One night old Lincoln went up to the car to his bed. He was guarding the car, he always did, all his life, he got under that car. And he came back to camp, and Manilla said, there is something wrong here. There must be something wrong. (Mother was very intuitive and seemed to have a "sixth sense" about things: Indians do, you know, and Mother was especially good at picking up on signs.) Well, I didn't pay too much attention and that day it had been drizzling rain a little bit. Manilla had taken all the clothes and washed them, then it started to rain, so we didn't have any dry clothes. So, I was sleeping in the complete nude. And old man Beck had been feeling kind of bad and Vance had gone up to stay with him. Anyhow, I could smell a skunk. Anyway, I got to smelling the skunk right after we went to bed. Now something had been licking the grease out of our skillets in the kitchen. It is the kitchen unless we are eating and then it becomes the dining room. So, I get up, nothing on, barefoot, pick up my .22 revolver and go out to shoot a skunk. Even if I had to move camp. That's what I told Manilla. I'd shoot it, even if we had to move camp. So, when I got out there with the flashlight, I had a 5 cell flashlight, and it seemed like in that dark country, that beam would just go out about 10 feet and stop.
>
> Anyway, I get out there flashing around, and all of a sudden, I see the bear – nice size brown bear. So, I rush back in, put my shoes on, and pick up the 30/30 rifle and

*go back out to assert my authority on this poor bear. But the only authority I could hit on was the rear end, and I didn't want to hit a bear in the rear end in that darkness. And besides, he was walking away. So, I thought, missed a bear, and now that you know we are here, you won't be back, I hope. And the next morning, I get up to go mining, pretty soon, here comes Manilla, Elizabeth Anne, the dog and the rifle.*

*"Where have you been," I say.*

*"Well, I was tracking the bear down, I thought I would shoot him if I could get him," Manilla answered. Umm Boy! If you shoot a bear, wound him, the first shot probably won't kill him. You've got a dog that is probably going to attack the bear. You got a bear that is going to attack you and attack Elizabeth Anne. Don't ever do that. Well, that's the way it goes.*

*Anyhow, she had tracked the bear. He went through camp, on down to the river banks, on further down the river and swam across apparently. His tracks ended in the water and didn't show up anywhere else, so I guess he was just a roving bear.*

I find this last bit about my mother wanting to shoot the bear a little farfetched on my father's part. I'm sure he was concerned and upset when he discovered that a dog, a five-year-old child, and a woman with a rifle were tracking the bear and I suspect he put his own spin on it.

I remember our tracking the bear. When we had cleaned up after breakfast, Mother got the 30/30 out and loaded it. She put some extra shells in her pocket, got the leash out and put it on old Lincoln and said, "Come on, Elizabeth Anne, let's go track that bear."

Now Mother was a good tracker. She could track almost anything over any kind of ground. It wasn't really that hard if you knew what you were doing. When I was really little she started teaching me to identify different kinds of animal prints and droppings. The direction the animals were moving, for example. She taught me to look at things like how recent the prints or droppings were which could give me an idea of how long ago the animal had been there. There were lots of other things you could tell from prints and droppings. She also taught me how to track when there weren't any tracks at all like over rock or hard ground. Then you look for subtler indications like a broken twig, a rock that's been moved, scratches on the rock or hairs on bushes. If there's none of that then you move to feel and intuition plus your knowledge and that worked, too. Years later when I had children of my own and our horses got out, I tracked them over several miles of unfamiliar and pretty tough terrain (my husband thought I was nuts) and I found them. I was grateful for all those lessons learned earlier. My mother was pretty big on what she called "skills of living." They could range from tracking and knowing how to survive in or live off the woods to swimming to shooting a rifle. They also included driving (when I was older – she had me driving by age 9 or 10 – "just in case") to climbing a tree. My dad sort of balked at the climbing of trees (he was a bit pudgy and more intellectually than athletically inclined.) He thought I would grow up to be a tomboy. Mother saw nothing wrong with that if doing everything and being able to take care of myself meant being a tomboy. Her favorite argument was, "Well, if Elizabeth Anne is in the middle of a big pasture and a mad bull charges her and there's nothing there but a tree, don't you want her to be able to climb a tree?" That would shut him up every time.

Let me say something about handling a gun. Both my parents believed that I should know about guns. First of all, guns aren't toys. I had a toy gun and it was just a toy. I knew that. They knew that I knew that. Real guns were not toys and should never be played with. Secondly, you should never, never point a gun at anyone, even in jest. It was just not to be done, period. You should always keep the safety on except when you are actually shooting, or ready to shoot of course. If something unexpected pops up, like a bear, it takes only a flick of the finger to release the safety. My parents said, "It's always an empty gun that kills people." Also, you should never keep a loaded gun around and never keep the shells where the gun was and both should be locked up when possible or kept in a safe place. Guns should always be pointed down when walking with them. They showed me how to crook a rifle in my arm so it was safe. Whenever going over a fence the gun should be placed on the ground and you should go through or over the fence and then pull the gun through butt first. After I learned all of that, this approach to handling guns made sense to me and then I learned to shoot. We were a family that always had guns around, as I said, and guns were never given to any of us until we learned the "proper respect" for them, were excellent shots and knew about the proper handling of guns. I was given my first rifle when I was twelve years old and outshot all my uncles at target practice. Boy, was I proud of that gun. It was a .22 single shot bolt action. I still have that gun.

Mother was much more at home in the woods than Daddy. He liked math and science more. Mother and Daddy often didn't see eye-to-eye about things so I was lucky to have both views to test out for myself.

Anyway, I was excited about tracking that bear. We were lucky it had rained the day before and the ground was wet so that made tracking easy. Mother and I both studied the bear's prints very carefully. She said when we got to know these California bears better, we could tell a lot about them from their prints. Mother said that looking at the tracks, it didn't seem that all our commotion had scared him much. He wasn't hurrying to get out of there <u>and</u> it was clear that he wanted to get far away from us. I don't suppose the bacon grease was worth being around humans to him. We followed him quite aways. I thought any minute we might run into him but we never did. Finally, his tracks disappeared into the river. Mother seemed relieved and satisfied. Then we went back and reported to Daddy and Vance. Daddy was upset. Mother didn't seem bothered by that. We then cleaned up after breakfast, as we had spent almost the whole morning tracking the bear. That was quite a morning.

The more I think about this entire incident, the more I believe Mother never intended to shoot the bear. She took the gun along for protection. It was not an aggressive but a defensive move on her part.

First of all, my mother didn't like to kill anything. She even thought we should catch flies and put them outside not killing them, when we lived in a house. She had a special rapport with animals and they would do almost anything for her. She had a unique form of communication with them. She also almost always knew what was wrong with them and how to heal them. The wounded animals found their way to her. We had a mini animal hospital going at our place almost all the time. When I was older, she used to go big-game hunting with my father. When she went with him, she didn't even want to carry a gun. She said her hunting was with her eyes. Daddy insisted that she carry a gun for two reasons: 1) so she could back him up if he were hurt or incapacitated or; 2) if he killed two deer or elk and he used her tag, (which they sometimes did to have game for winter) she would be there with her gun. So, sometimes she capitulated and she didn't like it. One time, years later, Daddy killed a bear while hunting in Montana. Mother was with him and I don't think she ever got over seeing and hearing that bear die. She said it fought to live and then let out a loud groan that ricocheted throughout the mountains as it fell dead. That sound and that image haunted her the rest of her life. She never would eat a bit of that meat. She would cook it for us and canned a bunch of it so we would have it, but she would never touch it. Besides, if she were going out to kill that bear in California she wouldn't have dragged Lincoln and me along.

This is what I think was going on in her mind although she never said. I think she was worried about the camp being safe now that there was a bear around. She was especially concerned about Lincoln and me. She was afraid to leave me alone in camp in case the bear was still around and she needed to know about that bear. She didn't want to frighten us so she made it a teaching game. She put a leash on Lincoln so he wouldn't force a confrontation. She kept me close all the time. I believe that she was confident that she could bring the bear down if she had to to protect us and she didn't want to. Her best-case scenario was that the bear was gone and since it had swum across the river, she was convinced the camp was safe again and Lincoln and I could have our freedom. For all I know, Mother may have told the bear to go on and get out of here that it wasn't welcome and we'd have to kill it if it hung around. She might just have been checking to make sure it got the message. And it had! Mother could do lots of things other people couldn't do.

So that was probably the most exciting night we had in camp our entire time there and I slept through it. I'm sure glad that bear didn't come into our tent. I'd of probably slept through that, too.

## Frenchy

Frenchy was without a doubt one of the most interesting characters I have ever met in my entire life. In fact, I can't think of any more interesting or anyone more of a character. As a five-year-old, I had nothing but utter fascination for him. I had never met someone from another country before, nor had my parents.

Daddy describes our first ever encounter with Frenchy (everyone called him "Frenchy" because he was from France).

> On the way down the Klamath River Road, when we first came in was the first time we saw Frenchy. He was coming up out of the river carrying a great big travel net all folded up. This travel net was something that was allowed out there. You could put this travel net in the river and catch certain fish. The Klamath River bank is awful hard to climb with a travel net we found out, so we stopped to help him.

*He says, "No, I'll carry it right on up," which he did.*

*We offered to give him a ride and carry the travel net on top of the trailer, which he accepted. I went around to pick it up to load it on the trailer and I couldn't lift the thing. Vance came behind there and he couldn't lift it. So the two of us put it up on the trailer. Yet, he was carrying it across his shoulder, up this steep bank with no problem at all. Some guy! Of course Vance and I were a little soft, especially my doing the work I was doing. I wasn't very husky or muscular. I was fat.*

When I first saw Frenchy, I had never seen anything like him. He had a strange, navy blue thing on his head that sort of slouched over to one side. Mother later told me it was called a beret! I had never seen a man wear anything like that and I knew he couldn't be a woman because he was too strong and lean and wiry. He had a regular shirt and pants, and the pant legs and shirt sleeves were rolled up showing sinewy, lean, tanned, muscular arms and legs. But what on earth was that around his waist? I tried to whisper and ask Mother since I was sitting on her lap in order to make room for him to sit in the back seat with Vance and Lincoln. Mother kept shushing me and whispering to me not to be impolite by asking questions about him. Whatever it was he had around his waist was black, wide and silky looking. Mother later told me it was like a sash or cummerbund whatever that meant! When I got to know Frenchy better and didn't think he would mind, I asked him and he told me that it was something he learned to wear in the French Foreign Legion and he had gotten used to wearing it because it was really sensible. One time when we were at his cabin, he showed me how he put it on. He tied one end to the bedpost (I'm not quite sure how he did that) and then he pulled it out until it was tight. It was so long it reached almost the whole length of his cabin – of course, his cabin wasn't very big. He would hold it right in the middle of his body with one hand, put his other hand up in the air and roll up tight to the bed post, then he would loosen that end from the bed post and tuck it in. He let me feel how tight it was. He said that it was very comfortable and a great back support. He reckoned if more men knew about them, more would wear them. But, I'm getting ahead of myself.

Frenchy was not tall. He was not short either. I guess he was about medium if a little on the short side. He was not bad looking and he wasn't what I would call good looking either. He had a face you would remember especially with that beret perched on it. His skin was dark olive. It would probably have been closer to the color of Mother's if he hadn't been in the sun all the time. His hair was black – what I could see of it under the beret. He was clean-shaven with a long, almost hooked nose with blue eyes set on either side of it. His face was thin. In fact, his whole body was thin. My parents called him wiry and swore there wasn't a spare ounce of fat anywhere on him. Everything about him seemed strong. Everybody who knew him said that he was very private and independent – a loner they said. But once we got to know him you couldn't have wished for a better friend.

He lived in a little cabin/shack up above the road on the other side of the road and about a mile away from Mr. Beck. We often dropped by his cabin when we picked up things for him in town. His cabin was very simple and neat as a pin. He had one of those old cast-iron bedsteads like my Grandma Reed had which was painted white like hers. The bed was over against the far, right corner when you entered the door. The bed was always carefully made with a quilt on top. His cabin was only one room. On the other side of the cabin from the bed was a table and chairs. Just to the left inside the door was a wood stove obviously used for heating and cooking. There was a rocking chair by the stove and shelves behind it. There was a type of counter with a dishpan, wash pan, a bucket of water and a place to cook. Above your head running all around his cabin were two shelves with cans of stored goods, tools and various kinds of equipment on them. The cabin was pretty sparse, and as I say, pretty simple. It had lots of light and a warm glow to it when the fire was lit. I felt comfortable there. I knew that he had built the cabin and everything in it himself except the stove and bed.

He became good friends with Daddy and Vance – all of us for that matter – and I think he felt more comfortable with the men. That was just my impression and how it looked to me.

Daddy and Vance found out that his name was Eugene De Vove (or De Fove). He and a friend had deserted from the French Foreign Legion somewhere in Africa – Morocco or someplace. I just knew it was far, far away. There was something mysterious about his being in the French Foreign Legion. The grown-ups acted a little funny about this like I wasn't supposed to hear, which was unusual since I was in on almost everything – or so I thought. Of course, this secrecy just made me more curious so I listened more carefully. I got the impression that the French Foreign Legion was like jail or something and he had been sent there because he had killed someone – accidentally, of course. My parents seemed to be sure that it was accidental – "self defense" – I heard them say one night in hushed tones. It was like a tragic story. Because he had deserted – that means run off without permission – he could never go back to France. I had a lot of daydreams about his never being able to go back to his home, his family, his friends. What if he had a sweetheart there and could never see her again – ever? It seemed like one of the saddest things I had ever heard. There seemed to be a sadness in his eyes sometimes when I was watching him. I never asked him about it.

Daddy said that he had worked as a sailor after he had deserted. And then he had come to the Klamath River. I guess he was like hiding out there. We had outlaws hiding out in Oklahoma so I knew what that meant.

One day, he and Daddy got talking. It turned out that he had graduated from the Sorbonne in Paris in electrical engineering. I think that's why he and Daddy hit it off so well. Daddy loved electronics and would talk for hours with anyone who understood him and could talk to him. He was pretty smart in electronics and Frenchy, it seems, could go him one for one and sometimes better. Daddy loved that. I think Daddy and Vance tried to fix him up with some kind of electronics work he could do. I don't know whatever came of that. He and Daddy seemed to respect and admire one another. And, although Frenchy liked and was nice to the rest of us, he and Daddy shared something unique. They were special friends. I liked to sit around and just listen to them talk with each other even when I didn't always understand what they were talking about.

Frenchy got so he would drop by our camp often and we went to his cabin, too. It was fun to listen to him talk. When he was speaking English, which he had to with us, he had an accent which was real different from anything I had ever heard before. Sometimes, he would stop to look around for just the right English word to use. You could almost see his mind searching to find the best descriptive word. Daddy said he spoke several languages, French, English, and Portuguese. I never met anyone like that before. All-in-all he was one of the most interesting people I had ever met. He wasn't warm and quiet and comfortable like Mr. Beck. He was a different kind of person entirely. Like I said, he didn't seem too comfortable around women. He seemed shy around Mother but she would loosen him up. Who could resist a woman who never met a stranger?

Frenchy seemed even more uncomfortable with a little girl than he did with Mother. He just seemed like he didn't quite know what to do with me. I kinda got a kick out of that. Sometimes, when people don't know what to do with you, you just sort of have to take charge and treat them normal-like, you know, like everything's all right and just normal and they'll start to believe it. That's what I did with Frenchy and we became pretty good friends. I sure was interested in everything he had to say.

Daddy said that Frenchy was the only white man who could swim the Klamath River. Imagine that! Swimming the Klamath River! Cars couldn't even survive it. I guess the Indians could do it and, according to Mother and Daddy, did it all the time. After all, it was their land and their place and they knew what to do with the land and the river. But the only way white people could get across was with a cable strung over the river or a bridge. It seemed like there were a lot of things that Indians did that white people couldn't do from what I could see. Maybe Frenchy had become like an Indian. Daddy said that Frenchy really loved the land and that country. When Daddy said that about Frenchy, something changed. It's like something became real quiet and kinda holy – like in church or in a big forest. Tears would come to Daddy's eyes and to mine, too. And, I know that there was something real, real special in the way Frenchy loved that land. It's like he and the land were connected. No, it was more than that . . . It was like he and the land were one. Maybe that's why he didn't need a wife or a family. Maybe the land was his sweetheart, his family, and his company. Maybe the land was enough. You know, after that talk with Daddy, I never felt sad around Frenchy any more. I had a hint that there was something bigger than wife, kids, family and so on. Maybe they were just a small part of things but the land and the water – they were part of something much, much bigger and Frenchy had a hold of whatever that was. After that, I was able to feel a kind of peace and quiet in Frenchy. I liked being around Frenchy and just feeling that quiet. We got to be even better friends after that and a lot of times I just sat quiet with him like I did with Mr. Beck.

Now back to his swimming the river. I guess he did all kinds of things on the other side of the river. There were no white people or houses over there. I heard that there were Indians that lived over there. I never saw any or anything but I heard that. Frenchy said that there was really good hunting and fishing across the river. There was lots of game and lots of fish and it hadn't been over-hunted or over-fished so I guess he swam over there to hunt and fish. I don't know. I do know that one of the reasons he swam the river was to help white folks when they wanted to put a cable across the river. He would swim the river with a big old rope swung along over one shoulder. That rope must've been pretty heavy itself. The rope was attached to a cable on our side of the river. When he got to the other side, he would pull the cable over and attach it to the other side. Then people could put a little cart-like thing on it and go across the river. It must have been a lot of work, swimming that river with that heavy rope, pulling that steel cable across and then fixing it on the other side. I'm not quite sure how he did it. But Daddy told me about it so it must be true.

Daddy had lots of other things he remembered about Frenchy.

*Frenchy came down, he never did like our sluice box because we were running great big rocks and everything else down it. He kept telling us we were losing our gold. But, we had quite a long sluice box and we had rugs in it and we could always tell if we were losing gold out of it because there would be gold down at the tail end of the sluice. And, in that tail end section we hardly picked up any gold or black sand either one . . . So, we didn't think we were losing anything. Maybe that is where our fortune went, I don't know.[27]*

*One day Frenchy came down and we told him about the bear.*

*He said, "Oh, come up and get some honey and smear it here and there and yonder in a tree. Maybe he'll come back and we'll have some bear meat."*

*Frenchy said when he hunted bear, he had two ways of doing that.*

*If the bear was hibernating, he would go in and feel around and find the bear. If that bear was good and fat, he would shoot it in the head and drag it out. He would shoot it in the head with a .38 pistol. He was the only guy I ever saw that could take a gun out, throw a can on the ground and just keep it dancing for six shots. He was a good shot.*

---

[27] One can get a hint of my father's stubbornness here. Of course Frenchy had more experience in gold mining than my dad did. But my dad had sat down and "worked this out" in his mind. When it came to anything mechanical or electronic, and when he had "worked it out," he was pretty sure that he was right and – he usually was. Frenchy would have had to demonstrate to my father that he knew a better way and then – my father would have shifted. If we had been able to stay there longer, this may have happened. This was one of the things my dad liked about Frenchy. Frenchy was as smart as my dad was – in the same areas of expertise. My mother was as intelligent as my father and she had her own areas of expertise that were completely different from my father's which made them a good pair.

His other way was to kill the bear when it was eating bear berries. There are trees out there in California – we called them bear berries. I don't know the scientific name for them. Bears climbed up these trees – they are not a tree really, just a tall bush is what they are. I mean a tall, scrub brush bush – Anyway, the bear would crawl up there and start eating these berries and Frenchy would go looking for him. Now he had a .12-gauge shotgun, single shot. He would shoot the bear with a shotgun.

Vance says, "But what if the first shot doesn't kill him?"

"I always have an extra shotgun shell in my mouth that I can put in right quick."

I don't know if the first shot didn't kill all of them, but at least the second shot must have because he was still around!

Anyway, back to the bear hunt. We went up to his cabin. He had a shelf all around the cabin just about as high as he could reach and cans all lined up on it. So he was going around tipping each can, a lot of them were empty. He came to one and pulled it down.

"Here's some honey," he says.

Well there wasn't very much in it and we knew Frenchy did not use sugar – he used honey for all his sweetening – and we didn't want to take it.

He says, "I got a whole 'nother gallon up there," pointing to this can. He finally talked us into taking it. We put a little out on the trees but we didn't want to use his honey up. The fact was that when he wasn't looking and was talking, I went over and tipped that can. It was completely empty. Frenchy was like that. He'd do anything for anybody. He had a heart of gold when you got to know him. I guess he was just a little cautious with strangers at first. He sure didn't seem like any "loner" to us once we got to know him. He came down to our camp a lot and we were always welcome in his cabin.

*I wanted to tell you about the lentils. Now, being a Frenchman, they eat horse meat over there.[28] Every fall he'd cure a horse and put it in his locker.*

*So one day Frenchy brought some lentils with some cured ham in it. Well, I could see that it was more or less ham and Vance thought it was ham. Frenchy said it was ham. We all had our little doubt about it. Manilla had a big doubt about it. We did eat some of those lentils. I don't recall if Manilla ate much of 'em or not, but Vance and I ate some. That was my first taste of lentils. I had not eaten them before.[29]*

Frenchy was around our camp a lot. He frequently brought over some bread or something he had made and he often ate with us. He sorta became like a member of the family, I guess. People were always becoming like a member of our family. That's how we were. Mother always said that if you think about it, everyone is really "family" anyway. He would also drop by and talk to the men at the sluice box or stay and sit around the fire at night and talk or tell stories. I felt kinda sorry for him when we would all go to bed and he'd still have to walk home alone. Anyway, it was one of those times when we were sitting around one night talking that he told us about Indian Hop Mountain.

---

[28] I don't know where my dad got this idea and I assume he got it from Frenchy although I have never heard it when I was in France – whatever!

[29] You can bet my mother didn't eat any of those lentils or that "ham!" She wouldn't go near it if she thought there were any possibility that it had horsemeat in it. She always said that she'd just as soon eat a hunk of human as a piece of horse – much rather, I reckon. Horses were sacred and her friends. You wouldn't eat a piece of a friend now, would you? So, Mother wouldn't taste anything that she thought might be horse. She was, however, fascinated with the lentils. We didn't have anything like lentils in Oklahoma and Arkansas in the 1930's as far as we knew. Mother was always interested in any new food and eager to try it out (except horsemeat, of course). During the war, she took a course on "variety meats" to help with the war effort – brains, kidney, heart, tripe – these didn't go over too well but she kept trying. Anyway, she picked Frenchy's brains about cooking lentils and they have been a part of our family food ever since. As I remember, cooking was one of the ways Frenchy and my mother connected.

# Indian Hop Mountain

(I find it interesting that my father never mentioned this little episode in the things he remembers about our time on the Klamath River. Perhaps you'll see why when you read the telling.)[30]

"H'es enione told youz about at zee Endian Hop Mounteen?" Frenchy asked one night out of the blue. We all grew silent as a sense of mystery and suspense hung in the air.

"I'eem not seeprized," he continued, not waiting for an answer when it was obvious that one was not coming. "Eem not seeprized a beet. Naught meeny people know about eet," he said lowering his voice just enough that we were sure some secret was about to be revealed and then pausing very, very effectively.

"Well, are you going to tell us about it or just let us sit here in suspense?" my daddy teased.

"Endian Hop Mounteen eese on ze other side of zee reever," Frenchy said. "Oh, of course zee eendians know about eet but most whyeet folks don't. Zee Eendians keep eet secret like. Eeef you know what eeh mean."

At this point, we were all leaning forward, straining to hear, not wanting to miss a word. It was like Frenchy was afraid that there were spies in the trees or bushes that might find out what he was telling us and we'd all be in trouble or ruin something if this secret got out. It was as if only very special people were allowed to know about this place and we were about to be let in on one of the most mysterious secrets of the whole Klamath River. Frenchy was barely talking above a whisper at this point.

"Zeer ees theeese place that ees like no one had ever beeen zear. Eet ees just like what eet must uv been before zee whyeet peepil came."

We were all eyes and ears as we strained to hear and see him, for he talked with his voice and his hands.

He continued, "There ees noh trails except zee deeur trails. Zer ees this streem. Oh, mai, wee, zees streem. It ees zo bu-te-ful. Eet cascades down zee mountain, over zee rocks in bu-te-ful waterfalls. Eet is zee most bu-te-ful

---

[30] Please remember – we were from a small town on the Oklahoma/Arkansas border. We had never met anyone from another country who spoke another language before. Our naiveté was immense. When Frenchy told us this story, his accent was even stronger and more intense for us than later, after we had grown to know him, making these encounters with him more intriguing and mysterious for us. I have tried to convey the experience of the "mystery."

place I have seen on zah earth." His eyes sparkled as he talked about this magical place. His face softened and he had a hint of tears in his eyes. I felt like we were being led through a magic door into a wonderland that only existed way, way back in time. It's like we were being taken back to a place in time and space we could never have gone without Frenchy. He continued.

"Un oh, the water – may wee, zee water. Eet ees so creestal clear and magnif that eeech drop has rainbows een eet as eet falls over zee rocks. Zee rocks are worn smooth from zee rainbow water dancing on eeem."

I could see it. I could see it in my eyes when I closed them. I could see all these rainbows dancing in the water. I'll bet there were fairies and little people there too if they would let you see them. Frenchy had taken us all to another land, a magic land that only existed on the other side of the Klamath River.

"Ohn dat ees not all," he said with a big grin.

We leaned closer – there was more!

"Zee feesh, may wee, zee feesh."

"What about the fish?" I asked, hardly able to contain myself. Mother always said, "Elizabeth Anne, contain yourself!" when I was getting too excited or too loud. The way Frenchy was telling this story with so much mystery and so much wonder, he was making it sound like the most exciting place in the world.

"Zee feesh are zee beegist and zee fatest you have ever seen. Beeg fate trout just weeting to be caught. Zee can put in a beeer hook and pull one huge fish out after another. You don't need any bait. Zee feesh, zey will steerike at anything."

Imagine being able to catch fish and not having to wait and work at it! It sounded like heaven. And then he went on:

"Oh zee feesh. When you pull eet out, clean eet and cook it right then over zee fire eet is zee best the thing zee mouth has ever tasted. Eeet isee better than anything you could ever find in zee beest restaurant in Pari, France. Eet ees better than anything in zee world."

We all knew that what he said was true and we didn't even know about the best restaurants in Paris, France, or anywhere else for that matter. Frenchy sat there with his eyes gleaming and he seemed far away like he was across that river eating those fish.

"Yees sir," he said. "Wheen you teek a peece of dat feesh off zee bone with your feengers – careful now – not to burn zee feengers because eet ees hot, jeest off zee campfire." And he closes his eyes and reaches out with his fingers putting one hand out with the fingers curved like he's holding the stick he has just cooked the fish on and with the other hand cautiously feels the air and is clearly touching something gingerly before he breaks off a piece and slowly puts it in his mouth. (I could feel my mouth opening as he put the fish to his mouth). Then – a smile of pure ecstasy breaks across his face. He looks like he is in heaven! Our mouths are all watering – we can almost taste that fish. He waits for just a moment and then he says, "Oooh!" and smacks his lips, slowly licking around his lips with his tongue. At this point, we are fairly drooling (My mouth is watering as I write this.) and he methodically and very carefully – one-at-a-time – puts his thumb, and then his index finger, and then his next finger, in his mouth and slowly, slowly, licks each one to savor every taste of that fish. We were convinced. We were ready. I think we would have taken off that night if we could have.

Then he said, "Wait a meenute. Eee have no fineeshed."

What more could he have to say? How <u>could</u> there be anything more to say? We all leaned forward to be in on the last piece of information about this amazing place.

"Zee treep back is even beeter than zee feesh." He paused . . . slowly, very slowly . . . he leaned back – with a big smile on his face. "Eh . . . weel say no more."

It was just like the ups and downs on the road. He had taken us up – and we were waiting to drop down with the pit of our stomachs leaping into our mouths and he left us there – hanging – just hanging in the air. He grinned again, that charming, teasing grin of his and got up.

"Wee, eh guess eh beeter be going home for now," and off he went. I'll bet he waited just out of the circle of light to see our reaction.

"Oh, Daddy, can we go? Can we do it? Can we go to Indian Hop Mountain?"

"I don't see why not, Elizabeth Anne. Okay with you Manilla?"

Mother's eyes sparkled. "When should we go?" she asked.

I certainly hoped it was soon.

"Let's talk about it in the morning," Mother said. We all agreed. We were all exhausted from the suspense and the excitement of Indian Hop Mountain. As I fell asleep that night, I could just see those big fat trout in that rainbow water.

The next day, we decided we could go in two days. The decision made, there was a lot of activity in our camp. Vance wasn't going to go because Mr. Beck was still feeling a bit poorly and he would stay with him. Silver wouldn't go either, what with having to cross the river and then having to hike so far over rocks and things. He didn't like things like that too much so we didn't insist that he go with us. So, it would just be the four of us, Mother, Daddy, Lincoln and me. Daddy said that he would talk to Frenchy and get more information about what we needed to take and how we got there. We were all eager to see what we needed to do to get ready. We didn't want to miss any detail because it was such a special trip.

The next day, after breakfast, Daddy sat down to tell us what Frenchy had told him. "The most important thing Frenchy told me is don't take too much. You don't need much of anything and there's no reason to be weighed down with things you don't need. The other important thing Frenchy told me was we can do it in one day if we want to and I think that's a good idea for our first trip. We can always go back if we want to."

We all nodded in agreement. "This means it will be a long day but Frenchy thinks Elizabeth Anne is up to it."

Of course I was up to it! How dare he!

Frenchy had told my father that we should get up before dawn and eat a good breakfast. It would be cool in the morning and evening so we should take a good jacket. I liked my blue one with the pockets in case I needed extra things, found some special rocks or pine cones or something. We should take some snacks for food – not much because mostly we would be eating fish. We didn't need to take fishing rods or poles. All we needed was a line with a hook on it. That would be enough. We needed to wear our sturdy shoes with good socks and long pants. I was the only one who wore shorts anyway it seemed to me. Frenchy suggested that I might want to catch some grasshoppers and dig up some worms just in case the fish wanted some bait. Besides, it seemed only fair we give them something. I was eager to do that and it was decided that I should start in the afternoon so they would still be alive and fresh when we got to the place where the fish were. Vance would take us up to the cable car, show us how to use it and pick us up at the end of the day. Daddy would take care of the other things.

We each had a knapsack that we would carry on our backs. The knapsacks were made of tan canvas with leather straps and metal buckles. Mine wasn't very big and it was just about the size I needed. Mother's and Daddy's were bigger and they would carry the big stuff we needed. Mother always took along emergency things like a first-aid kit, a small blanket and stuff like that.

"You never know what we'll need," she always said. Daddy always said that he was afraid that her "extras" would make too much of a load but Mother said she'd carry it.

Daddy told us that Frenchy had said that if we got to the cable by six thirty or seven, then went across and hiked along the river to the place where it was good to go up Indian Hop Mountain, that should take us about an hour to an hour-and-a-half or so, depending . . . I never knew "depending" on what. If we looked up the mountain when we got across the river, we could see a lot of shale. Shale, I was told, was a lot of broken rock. It was something like the pieces of black slate we had in the rivers in the Ozarks only it was harder, more like granite, and a different color. Anyway, when we could see that we were past the shale, we should start up the mountain. That was a hard climb and should take two to three hours depending. There's that word again. I wondered if Frenchy meant depending on Manilla and Elizabeth Anne. We were in much better shape than Daddy. He said so himself. I made up my mind right there that I was going to keep up or die trying.

Then, when we hit the creek, if we just followed the creek up for about an hour, we'd have to cross it back and forth several times (we'd know where) and then we'd find that magical place with the big, deep pools that held those fat, juicy, lazy trout just waiting to be caught.

Lincoln and I talked it over on our way up to the landing and Mr. Beck's yard to catch grasshoppers and dig earth worms – that's where the most and the fattest ones were – in the garden – and we knew we could handle it. Mother had given me a peanut butter jar with holes punched in the lid for the grasshoppers – 'cause they moved around so much – and a smaller one for the worms. When I got to the top of the trail, there were grasshoppers everywhere and I started to catch them. It wasn't hard. I would just drop them in the jar and they would keep on hoppin'. I looked up and saw Mr. Beck waving me over.

"Whatcha got there?" he said.

"Grasshoppers," I said. "We're going fishin'."

"I hear you're going up to Indian Hop Mountain," he said.

I was so relieved. I didn't know if I was supposed to tell anyone about Indian Hop Mountain or not. It seemed like such a secret and I didn't know whether Frenchy wanted it told. Mr. Beck was my friend and I sure didn't want to lie to him either or even keep a secret from him. I hadn't lied. I'd said we were going fishing. That was the truth. Mother said never, never lie – you just don't always have to tell all the truth sometimes. I guess that was what I did.

Now that Mr. Beck knew, and I knew he knew, we had a lot to say to each other.

"I guess you must be pretty excited," he said.

"Oh, I am, Mr. Beck. I can hardly stand the waiting. It's been like waiting for the carnival to come to town after all the posters have been put up. But this is free and we're going to bring those big, juicy fish back for everyone. You, too, Mr. Beck. Daddy will clean them right away then we'll put them in those plastic bread bags and keep 'em in the cold water until we're ready to come back. Frenchy said the trip back wouldn't take that long."

Mr. Beck's eyes were shining. He seemed to be getting better.

"Do you have enough of those plastic bread bags?"

"I believe so. Mother always saves them."

"Well, I have some. I'll give you a few so you can have extra if you need them."

I'll bet Mr. Beck was sure looking forward to those fish.

"Lemme see that jar," Mr. Beck said. "My, my – you have it fixed up real nice with holes in the top and everything."

"Mother did that," I said.

"But you know what? That big jar full of grasshoppers is going to be pretty heavy to lug up that mountain. You keep on catching grasshoppers and I'll rummage around and see if I can come up with something better."

That's the way Mr. Beck was. He had been sick and everything, yet, he still wanted to help me. Pretty soon he came back with one of those tin cans with a lid on it.

"How about this?" he said. "It's got plenty of room and it's a lot lighter."

He already had punched holes in it so the grasshoppers could get air. It seemed like a special little can and I wouldn't have taken it if he hadn't already punched holes in it.

"You can take your shovel and dig worms in the garden. It's the best place to get them. You have to put dirt in the jar and keep it wet so they can crawl in and out. That'll keep them wet and wiggly. That's the way the fish like them."

I knew that, and I didn't take offence or anything 'cause I knew that he was just trying to help. When I had my worms and grasshoppers, I went up and thanked Mr. Beck and told him I'd see him later. I didn't think he'd be up when we left so I waved and yelled over my shoulder.

"We'll bring you some fish, Mr. Beck."

I was so excited I could hardly go to sleep. I carefully laid out everything I would need to take so I could hurry in the morning and crawled into bed and fell right asleep.

The next morning, I was sound asleep when Mother woke me. It was pitch dark. She shook me gently and said, "Come on, Elizabeth Anne, it's time to get up." She had a flashlight so I could see where my things were. Daddy was lighting the lantern over the table. We ate, packed our knapsacks and headed up the trail. Lincoln heard us coming and greeted us with a wagging tail. We gave him his food right then and there. Vance came down from Mr. Beck's and we all loaded in the car and headed up to the cable that crossed the river. At this point, I had heard about the cable across the river and heard cables described and I had never actually seen one. What a shock! The cable was strung from a pole up high on the riverbank and it connected to another pole about the same height on the other side of the river. These poles were actually quite aways from the river. The cable hung down (to where it looked like from where we stood) awfully, dangerously close to the river. The thing we were going to go across the river in – I honestly didn't know what to call it – I had picked strawberries at one of those "pick 'em yourself" places with Mother and Daddy. They gave me a kind of carrier to use. It was made of wood, was about square, and had a little ridge all around it to hold in the strawberry baskets – it held nine, I think. Then, it had a piece of wood nailed on two opposite sides and a piece of round dowel that ran across it and was used as a handle. Then it was fastened to these two pieces of wood that stuck up. This "thing" also had a board across between the two pieces that stuck up straight – I don't explain very well. What I know as I looked at it was – terror. The whole contraption was being held by a rope that fastened to a ring on the pole that held the cable. Panic filled me. It was a strawberry carrier for heaven's sake! It was puny! It was little! How could anything like that take the four of us across the river? If I thought the roller coaster was bad, this was a hundred times worse (and any other big number I could think of) and we were going to swing out over the treacherous Klamath River on it. Mother looked pale; Lincoln was starting to shake, and I was ready to bolt for the car. If it hadn't been for that magic place, those big, fat, juicy easy-to-catch trout, and the secret that I still didn't know about coming back, I would have high-tailed it right back to the camp. I'm sure Lincoln would have been right on my heels. Vance said that he had done it before (crossed in the strawberry carrier) and it was fine. But he'd been the one who had taken me on the roller coaster too. I was clear that he couldn't be trusted in things like this and seemed to "have no judgment" at all as Mother put it. I looked to Daddy, he looked a bit green but determined. I looked to Mother, she looked like if Lincoln and I ran, she would be right behind us. Vance was explaining to Daddy how it worked.

"It's a lot sturdier than it looks. You'll see. I've seen two big burly men and all their equipment go across in this and it was just fine."

"Who's he trying to convince?" I said under my breath.

"Hmm," said Daddy.

Mother, who almost always had something to say, was perfectly silent.

"What you do is this. You pull in the rope like this and pull in the cable car (Cable car! cable car! I don't see any cable CAR) like this," as he slowly pulls that thing closer with the rope that ties it to the pole. "When you get it to the pole you put on the brake to hold it here while you get loaded," (Brake? Brake? It looks like a wedge of wood to me!) "Then," he continued. "You load in and pull it back just a little to loosen the 'brake'. You take it out and away you go sailing across the river." (I should have taken off when I first had the idea). "Gravity should take you about three-quarters of the way across the river. Then, Virgil will have to pull you hand-over-hand the rest of the way. That's what those gloves there on the floor of the cable car are for."

I looked at the thing. Sure 'nuf, there were two pairs of old, heavy leather gloves on the floor of the thing. They were worn, and looked a bit stiff with the fingers curled up – permanently – probably from pulling people across the Klamath River. It was okay to leave those gloves there on the "thing." Nobody would take them and they were there if anybody needed them. (I couldn't imagine many people wanted to get in this "thing" anyway.) That's the way things were down on the Klamath River. People looked out for one another. I stood there and wondered if Frenchy had in his time estimates figured about two hours trying to get up courage to get on that thing. Where was he anyway?

Vance said, "Okay, let's get you loaded up."

Nobody moved. I wondered if I had put too much in my knapsack. Maybe that would make it too heavy. Maybe I needed to re-pack and lighten it. I looked at Mother and Daddy. Could I trust them? They had not shown good judgment (Mother's phrase) about the roller coaster when they let me go on it.

"Let's go," said Vance. "Put Lincoln in first and tie his leash to the pole there, tight so he won't jump." (Won't jump – won't jump – into that river – who did he think Lincoln was?!) He took his leash and said, "Come on, Lincoln." Lincoln didn't budge. He was not moving and he was not getting into that thing. Daddy picked him up and Lincoln was shaking like a leaf.

"He didn't know what he was getting into when he joined this family," my mother always said. Neither did I!

"Elizabeth Anne and Lincoln will have to sit on the floor and Manilla you and Virgil can sit on the bench. Manilla you can help Virgil hand-over-hand it on the other side or not as you wish."

Mother looked at Vance like he must be completely insane and I was sure we all were. Then, Daddy picked me up and sat me down by Lincoln. The "thing" swayed every time anyone wiggled. Lincoln couldn't help his shaking but we both vowed not to move a muscle.

Then, Mother and Daddy started to get in while Vance held the "thing." My opinion was that this thing was definitely not safe. In my quick evaluation of the situation, it was a distinct possibility that the entire bottom would fall out right in the middle of the river. Lincoln might be okay 'cause he could hang by his leash. Mother and Daddy would be okay because they were on the bench – but what about me? Right then and there I determined to put one hand under Daddy, one under Mother and the other on the floor so I was touching Lincoln. Then, we would both feel safe. (To this day, I still have a visual memory of having three hands. I don't know how I did it and I would swear I had three hands. We can do powerful things when we are that terrified.)

Vance said, "Okay now, this'll be fun. I'll hold the car back and Virgil pull out the break."

Before I knew what was happening, we were off careening across the river. I can't say I enjoyed it. I can't say anything. I have some memory of the river seeming very close. I remember the cable kind of bouncing up and down and I was terrified we all would be flung out. (There were no seat belts!) Then we reached the end and started to roll back a little. What if Daddy couldn't hand-over-hand us and we just hung over the river forever? I was sure Frenchy would swim the river and save us. That thought gave me little comfort at that point. Mother was pale as milk and silent as a graveyard.

Daddy did the hand-over-hand thing and we reached the other side. He put on the brake, and lifted me out. Never, even after the roller coaster, have I been so glad to have land under my feet. I was so excited to still be alive. Lincoln felt the same way. Daddy lifted him out and took off his leash and Lincoln ran around and around barking and whining. Mother was where she had been, clutching the handle and looking straight ahead. I guess she knew now what it was like to be on that roller coaster. Daddy said, "Come on, Manilla," and slowly got her unglued from the thing. We were so relieved to be across the river, on the ground and walking, that no one dared to mention that later in the day the only way back across the river would be on the "thing."

We walked along the river until Daddy, from what Frenchy had told him, decided it was time to "head up the mountain." Frenchy was right. It was a hard climb. I was gonna prove we weren't going to have to stop because of me. Lincoln agreed so we just kept going. Every once-in-a-while Daddy or Mother would call a stop and Lincoln and I were grateful. We never complained though. We would drink some water and water Lincoln. One time we had a snack. Mother had brought some oranges and sandwiches "just in case." She did "just in case" a lot and we often had an "in case." Those oranges and sandwiches sure tasted good. We'd been up a long time. As we climbed higher and higher we would stop to look out over the river and the valley. It was so beautiful. The river got farther and farther away like a trickle down there and it was like we had an eagle-eye view. Pretty soon we were at the creek and then – everything changed.

We moved into a thick, dark, silent forest. It was as if we had passed through an invisible curtain. We were entering Frenchy's magic world. There were moss and needles on the ground. The silence seemed old, like Mr. Beck. The only sound was the sound of the stream and it was more than a stream. It was rainbows and fairies and little people and whispers. Frenchy was right. This was a different world . . . like a world that had been here and gone somewhere else . . . somewhere we couldn't get to very often anymore. We all felt it as we walked along the stream. No one said anything. It was – like – holy or something – like God had said, "Hush," and this place had been the only one to hear it and had hushed. I loved it there! We all whispered.

We walked up the stream and then we came to the first place where we had to ford the stream. We just couldn't go any farther on our side. I was excited and pulled off my cowboy boots and socks. That felt good. I inched closer to the water and stuck my feet in. The water was cold and it felt like it had bubbles or something in it. The climb up the mountain had been hot and I loved putting my feet in that cool, cool water. Daddy and Mother decided that the stream was too fast and too deep for Lincoln and me to wade. I was disappointed. I thought I was going to be able to get my clothes wet like Daddy. First Daddy carried Lincoln over and then came back for me. Lincoln didn't like being carried across the stream. He got "that look" on his face and his tail went straight down and dragged in the water. Mother waded across with Daddy standing in the middle giving her a hand and then it was my turn. Daddy stooped down with his back to me and told me to put my arms around his neck and he would carry me piggyback. I kept trying to drop my right foot in the water as we crossed. He kept saying "Sit up straight, Elizabeth Anne." I just wanted to get in that water. We hiked farther and forded several more times and then we were there.

We knew it was the right place the minute we saw it. The forest was cool and silent with an occasional birdcall. There were several big, quiet, deep pools, each spilling into the next one in a symphony of cascading waterfalls. Daddy said to be careful because the pools were much deeper than they looked. The water was crystal clear, like it was there and not there at the same time. I reckoned that these pools were the closest I had seen to the crystal clear spring-fed creeks of the Ozarks. I was sure the term crystal clear had been made up to describe those Ozark streams. And, wonder of wonders, in each pool floating just above the bottom and moving ever so slightly so as not to get carried with the current, were the biggest, fattest, laziest old trout I had ever seen. There were tons of them just lounging in that rainbow water. My mouth started to water remembering what Frenchy had said about eating them and how good they tasted. We hadn't had any fish in a while. We ate a lot of fish in the Ozarks.

We sort of fooled around a bit, exploring and just being glad to be there. The ferns on the banks of the stream were so big and so green they fairly glowed in a magical green. It was so quiet and so peaceful there I almost felt like I could fall asleep but there was too much to do (I did feel like the worries brought up by the "thing" fell asleep there. Not once did I think about the trip back). I stuffed some small rocks in my pocket to have from this place. I clamored over the big rocks and played in the shallows. It was a place you could stay for a long time. Slowly, Mother started to unpack her knapsack. She had one orange left, one whole sandwich, the corn meal and bacon grease for the fish if we wanted to fry them or we could add it to the corn meal and roll them in it for flavor – not that I thought those fish needed flavor. Frenchy said they were the best in the world and I just knew he was right. She also unloaded a tobacco tin filled with matches and the fixin's for "stick bread." Did I love stick bread! To make stick bread was easy. You just mixed some flour and salt and then added a little water – not too much! The dough needed to be stiff, Mother said. Sometimes Mother added baking powder or a little baking soda but you really didn't need it. Then, you would mix the dough and kinda pat it out in a strip with your fingers. If it turned out sticky, you needed to add more flour. When you got it rolled out in a strip, you would wrap it around a stick and hold the stick over the fire and cook it. That's why it was called stick bread.

"Elizabeth Anne, you get your grasshoppers and worms out of your pack so Daddy can catch the fish. I'll start the fire so we have some nice coals to cook the fish and we'll have lunch. She had figured that stick bread and fish were probably all we needed for lunch since we would have all the fish we could eat. "Virgil, you go cut us some sticks for the stick bread."

We all "hupped-to" so we could add our piece to this glorious meal. It was early afternoon and we were all beginning to feel our stomachs. Even old Lincoln seemed hungry. He was looking forward to these fish as much as we were. He always would eat whatever we did.

Daddy went to his knapsack to get his knife out of his tackle box so he could cut and strip some branches. He took an awfully long time looking through his knapsack. Mother and I had everything else ready. The fire was on a big flat rock and burning well. The stick bread was all ready to mix, but we wouldn't add the water and cook it until the fish were almost ready.

Mother said, "If you want to go ahead and get some fish, Virgil, give me the knife and I'll cut the sticks while you catch and clean the fish. Two of those should be more than enough for the four of us. They look almost as big as salmon."

Now Mother always carried a knife in her purse "in case we needed it" but she hadn't brought her purse to Indian Hop Mountain (why would she!) so she would have to use Daddy's from his tackle box. Then is when we heard it . . . the silence. Daddy's silence was thicker and heavier than anything that could come from those woods. We looked over and was he mad! Boy was he mad! I don't think I had ever seen him so mad. He was just sitting there in his wet pants with his arms laying over his knees and his forearms and his head hanging down and he was fuming. Mother and I looked at each other – and shrugged. We were a little nervous about saying anything.

"What's wrong, Virgil?" Mother asked.

"I don't <u>have</u> a knife," Daddy said.

"Oh, that's okay, Virgil. We'll get by," said Mother. "I can find some twigs we can use for stick bread "

"I forgot my tackle box," my dad growled. "We don't have any hooks."

Mother's and my eyes met. We knew in our heart of hearts that this would <u>not</u> be a good time to laugh. Daddy was furious. We might be killed. So we tried not to look at each other because if we did, we were sure to laugh and no telling what Daddy would do. Not that he'd ever done anything. But you know what I mean. What's funny to one person might not be funny to another. This was one of those times! For sure this was one of those times! So we both just turned away and waited a little while. We had taken two days to get ready, risked life and limb crossing the Klamath on that "thing." We had spent almost three hours getting up the hill, packing our knapsacks and then another hour to get to the magic place with the deep pools and the big fish, and Daddy had forgotten the fishhooks! You just had to laugh.

Just about the only thing we really needed was hooks. We could figure out something for almost anything else. But we sure needed those hooks to catch those fish. We didn't even have a knife to try to whittle a hook like the Indians did.

Mother and I turned our backs so Daddy couldn't see our faces and to let Daddy stew a while while we tried to figure something out. We searched our clothes to see if we had any safety pins. Sometimes we used safety pins until something could be sewed. Mother said that we could bend a safety pin into a hook. Mother reckoned if we could find one it might work. We didn't have one. We couldn't think of a thing.

Mother went over to Daddy. He was madder than I had ever seen him. He looked puffed up, he was so mad. It was like something was coming out of him even in his back and it seemed like it could be dangerous – whatever it was. I kept my distance so as not to disturb him – so did old Lincoln. I guess Lincoln felt it, too. Lincoln wasn't dumb. It seemed like Daddy might blow up. I'd never seen him blow up, but it seemed like he could this time and I didn't want to be the cause of it. In fact, I was sure glad that I hadn't been the one who forgot the fishhooks. I secretly suspected that if I had been the one who forgot them, he wouldn't be as mad at me as he was with himself. Mother put her hand on his shoulder. It must have felt kinda hot 'cause she pulled it back right away.

"Come on, Virgil," she said. "Let's all put our heads together and see if we can come up with something. We're all hungry so let's eat first and then we can think clearer. I have a can of beans I put in my knapsack (just in case.) I also stuck in one of those little can openers (just in case, of course). I'll mix a little corn meal and the bacon grease with the flour for the stick bread and we'll have a nice lunch. We'll save the sandwich and the orange for the trip back – just in case."

Daddy grunted and Mother and I got busy with lunch. I gathered a little more fuel for the fire to stir it up a bit. Mother mixed the stick bread, she put the beans in the skillet with a little more bacon grease for seasoning and produced these spoons from her knapsack. I wondered what else was in there. It was almost as good as her purse. We each broke off pieces of the stick bread dough, rolled it out with our hands, wound it around a stick and baked it over the fire. Mother and I took turns cooking extra for old Lincoln. He sure liked stick bread and beans. We did, too. The beans tasted so good warmed over our little campfire and the stick bread was wonderful. None of us ate as much as we could have and it was enough.

Then we sat down and tried to figure this one out. Clearly, Daddy had been trying to do this already – without much success, as Mother would say. Daddy wasn't talking much so Mother kinda took over.

"Let's see," she said. "We don't have any fishhooks, no safety pins, or anything like that to make fishhooks out of."

Daddy made a scowl and kinda jerked when she said that but she went on.

"The fish are in deep pools so we can't hand fish them – they need to be driven into shallow water for that. We could tear up our clothes and make a crude net. That might or might not work and I don't think that's a good idea. We could take scraps and make a seine and string it across the pools but we need hooks for that. We don't have a spear or anything to make one with or the kind of trees we need to do it." (We were surrounded by gigantic trees whose first limbs were miles up and very thick and heavy.)

"We don't have much time, an hour or hour-and-a-half at most and how would we clean the fish when we caught them? We might use a stick. I don't see any sharp rocks around. I think we're stuck . . . No fish!"

Mother had finally said those dreaded words! We would go home without any fish. It wasn't so bad for us but Vance, Frenchy and Mr. Beck were counting on us. We had been able to cross the river, climb that beautiful mountain and look out and then hike up to this wonderful, wonderful place like no place else ever and there was still the surprise. That was enough for us.

Then Mother said, "Maybe it's better this way. This place is so special partially because of the magnificent fish. Without even one of them, it wouldn't be so magical. Just look at them there so peaceful in the water, swishing their tails so slowly and suspended in that crystal clear water. Look at their beautiful colors and how they blend into shadow. They're part of this place. Maybe we weren't supposed to take some out."

Daddy didn't say anything. I kinda agreed with Mother. It was okay that we had no hooks. We were having a wonderful day. I think Daddy was so upset because he usually didn't do things like that. He was usually very careful about everything.

"Elizabeth Anne," Mother said. "You know, those grasshoppers and worms might not live captured like that until we get back to let them loose. Why don't you feed them to the fish? I think that would be okay. What do you think, Virgil?"

Again, another grunt. When I acted like that Mother said that I was holding onto my pout. I guess grownups did that, too. Sometimes it just felt good to hold on to a pout until you were good and ready to give it up (if it wasn't too long), Mother had said. It sorta cleans out the soul, if you know what I mean. We silently agreed to let Daddy hold onto his pout and we went off and fed the fish. We fed them in all the deep pools. That was great! They splashed, and darted and jumped. It was a regular fish show. I was glad we hadn't caught, killed, and eaten them. They were so alive and as frisky as a little, spring colt, only there were a bunch of them and more came when we were throwing grasshoppers and worms in the water. Those grasshoppers and worms sure made those fish happy. I guess they felt good about that.

Mother and I explored around a bit, we sat in the ferns, and watched the water. We lay on our backs and watched the trees swaying way up high and listened to the water. It was like we were letting that place seep into us, Mother said, so it would always be with us (she was right!). I even think we dozed a little. I went to a world that has been there for me to revisit in my dreams. After a while, Mother looked at her watch and said, "We better clean up our little camp and get going, Elizabeth Anne. We want to get across the river before dark." She sure was right on that one. I couldn't even imagine what it would be like crossing the river in that "thing" after dark and I sure didn't want to find out. We walked back to our little camp. The big pools were still there with the big trout in them and I guessed, thanks to Daddy, they'd stay there for a while. Daddy looked like he had a doze, too. Secretly I hoped so. Maybe he would be in a better mood. Lincoln seemed ready to go.

"Take the bean can and get some water to dowse the campfire," Mother told me. It looked like the fire was dead and we never took any chances. We didn't want to be the ones to start a forest fire and burn down this magical place! I dowsed the fire and Mother had dug a hole in the wet earth by the water. We carried the wet ashes and partially burned sticks and buried them in the damp hole just to be sure. Then she carried some water and used some pine needles to wash off the rock where the fire had been, so it looked like it had when we came. Mother put the empty bean can and top, the can opener, the spoons and the small skillet wrapped in plastic bread wrappers in her knapsack along with the sandwich and the orange. She had brought one folding cup, too, we discovered. Her knapsack looked much lighter than it had been on the way up. I put the tin can from the grasshoppers and the jar for the worms back in my knapsack along with my jacket. And we started back.

The trip back was easier. We were going downhill. Daddy still was grumpy, especially when fording the stream, so Lincoln and I were careful not to make it hard for him. We were very good. Mother seemed fine about having no fish. Lincoln and I were too. We were happy. When we got to the place where we left the stream, Daddy suggested that we stop to eat our sandwich and orange and have a good cold drink of this special water before we went on. I was a little nervous about not getting to the Klamath River before dark, but a drink and a bite to eat sounded good. We all shared the sandwich and Lincoln wasn't interested in the orange. It was juicy and sweet. As I drank the water from the stream, I closed my eyes and could still see the rainbow water and the magic place like Mother said I would (I can still see that place in my mind's eye today!) I was so glad she filled the metal canteen with that water when we left.

Then, Lincoln and I got up and started to go down the mountain the way we had come up. "Wait a minute, Elizabeth Anne," Daddy called. "Come on back, Lincoln." We both came running back.

"We're not going down that way. Now is the time for you to learn the secret of Indian Hop Mountain. Come on, follow me," he said.

It seemed like he was over his pouting fit and our daddy was back. I was so excited. What <u>was</u> the secret? He walked right out over the top of that shale field that we had gone around when we came up. We were right at the edge of the woods looking over nothing but rocks, rocks and more rocks. It was pretty steep and not straight down or anything.

"This is Indian Hop Mountain," he said.

I knew that.

"We can roller skate down,"[31] he said.

What on earth did he mean by that?

"Only we don't need roller skates and we don't need sidewalks." Now I was really confused. Mother was smiling.

"Frenchy told me how to do it," Daddy said. "You take a couple of running steps and then you just slide. You don't go straight down. That

---

[31] We didn't know anything about skiing at that time or I am sure he wouldn't have said "ski" down.

would be too dangerous. Go one direction and then turn around and go another going across and a little down on each one, zig-zagging. Here, I'll show you."

He took two big steps and just slid and then turned and did the same thing. It looked like fun. He came puffing back up the hill and said, "I'm sure you can do it. It's probably better to stay on your feet but if you don't, it's okay. You can slide on your bottom, too."

I knew I could do it.

"Here, let me take your hand for the first time."

I didn't really need to hold his hand but I guessed he'd feel better if I did and it sure was nice to have my daddy back.

"What about Lincoln?" I asked.

"Oh, he'll manage just fine," said Daddy.

So, off we go. We took off with Mother right behind us. I was screeching with joy. Daddy was laughing. Mother was laughing. I was laughing. Sometimes one of us would fall down and slide on our bottoms for a while and we would all laugh. Sometimes we were laughing so hard that we had to stop to catch our breath – not from the ride on the shale but from the laughing. Indian Hop Mountain had taken us almost three hours to climb and about fifteen minutes to come down! We collapsed at the bottom, huffing and puffing, laughing and crying we were laughing so hard. Everything was okay. We had had the perfect day we were expecting. We were all even sure that we could deal with that "thing" again if we had to and we had to!

We stopped to rest for awhile and caught our breath. We all were breathless from our trip down Indian Hop Mountain. We drank some of that water from the magic stream and hiked to the cable. Lincoln and I didn't even put up a struggle. We knew we had to do it and we did want to get back home to our camp.

When we were all loaded in and Daddy was ready to pull it back and release the "brake" under the pulley wheel, he said, "Don't look down, Elizabeth Anne." Believe me, I didn't.

Vance was there waiting. He look puzzled that our knapsack was so light when he loaded them in the car. When we told him about the fishhooks, he laughed and laughed until tears rolled down his cheeks. Daddy laughed with him.

"Next time," Vance said and all nodded tired heads in agreement. We dragged back to our camp tired, hungry and fishless. We had Spam sandwiches for dinner.

It was okay that Daddy forgot the fishhooks. We had a good time, anyway. I never did get to taste that fish. Yet, I kinda feel like I did taste it that night around the campfire when Frenchy first told us about Indian Hop Mountain.

(Now you can see why Daddy didn't mention the trip to Indian Hop Mountain in his memoirs.)

## The Wild Pig Incident

It was another one of those evenings around the campfire. Daddy and Vance got to telling about wild pig hunting. They had read about someone finding wild pig somewhere in Arizona and they got all excited about doing that sometime. They spent a lot of time talking about how mean and vicious the pigs were. "Why, you know those wild pigs are not like regular pigs. They're a different breed. They're vicious. I read where they usually hunt them with pig dogs and if those dogs aren't careful, they'll just take those tusks and those sharp front teeth and gut the dogs," said Vance.

"Yeah," chimed in Daddy. "Those dogs gotta be pretty smart and work together. Some of them have to be in back nipping at the pig's heels while the others try to rush him."

"Yeah, once the dogs get one treed, the pigs get pretty vicious. You can have ten dogs on that pig and he can take five of 'em out without batting an eye."

I sure didn't want Lincoln going wild pig hunting. I knew he would try to protect me no matter what but I didn't want him to get killed. Wild pig hunting didn't sound that great to me.

"You know, the ones in South America are supposed to be even more dangerous," said Daddy. "They can weigh up to five-hundred pounds and are really fast."

Mother didn't care much for those kinds of discussions and had gone to bed. I was scared and I still wanted to hear what they had to say.

"I hear those pigs aren't scared of anything," Vance said.

"They'll charge anything when they are cornered. They'll face a man with a gun with no fear at all and rip his leg wide open or worse," Daddy added.

"Yeah," said Vance, "and I guess it's even worse when they are wounded. I heard tell they ripped one fellow's guts right out . . . couldn't save him – just tore him to pieces."

"I read an article about some rich fellow from back East who went trophy hunting for wild boar in South America. He had all kinds of fancy equipment, big gun, 30/06, I believe. He'd hired a whole bunch of local people to carry his stuff, cook, scout and shoot – sort of like one of those safaris in Africa except this was in South America – and he got cornered by a wild boar and was torn to pieces. Yes, sir, I guess they had to send him home in pieces. Not much all those people he'd hired to hunt with him could do to save him. Those guys kept pumping shots into that big old boar and he just kept going until they were both dead. There was no stopping him."

"Yeah, Virgil, we ought to go down to Arizona and give it a try sometime. It should be exciting," Vance said.

"Yep, well, better go to bed. Busy day tomorrow. Come on Elizabeth Anne. It's past your bedtime."

"Goodnight Virgil."

"Goodnight Vance. Sleep well."

I hoped I never, never ran into a wild pig and if Daddy and Vance ever went wild pig hunting, they sure were not going to take Lincoln along to be a pig dog if I could help it.

The next morning was a usual morning around camp. After breakfast Mother and I were cleaning up and Daddy said, "I have to go up to the car to get some tools to fix the sluice box. Do you and Lincoln want to go with me, Elizabeth Anne?" Lincoln had come down from guarding the car and to get breakfast some time ago. "Okay if I take Elizabeth Anne and Lincoln, Manilla?"

"Of course, you go ahead, Elizabeth Anne. I'll finish up here," Mother said.

Off we went up the trail through the woods to the landing and Mr. Beck's. We went up in our usual fashion. Lincoln ran ahead. I ran after him and Daddy followed along, aways behind. The path, which was just a foot trail really, started at the end of the clearing where camp was and went off to the right through the thick forest. It was dark and cool on the path as there were no clearings until we got to the landing and the tall trees shaded and covered it all the way up. It got a bit lighter as we got closer to the landing as the sun hit it sooner and filtered through the trees. The path went uphill from the camp to the landing and was quite steep in places as the landing sat above the riverbed quite a bit higher than the camp. About halfway up there was a sharp turn to the left with a big tree on the right side so that if the trail from above went straight it would run right into that tree. It was impossible to see the path above the tree from the lower path and impossible to see the path below the tree from the upper path. As I said, on that day Lincoln had run on ahead of Daddy and me and I was running ahead of Daddy. As I neared the sharp curve, I could hear Lincoln barking on the upper trail. That was not unusual. He barked when he wanted to. He wasn't a "barker" for no reason and he did bark sometimes. I couldn't see what he was barking at until I came around the curve. I came running around the curve and there was Lincoln barking like a son-of-a-gun and nipping at the heels of a great, big pig that was squealing like crazy and charging right at me. I backed up against the tree. I could feel its rough bark on my back and I had nowhere to go. The pig was charging me. I let out a yelp and . . . froze. When the pig saw me, it veered off into the woods to the left of the tree and disappeared. Daddy had heard me scream and came galloping up the path. He and Lincoln, who had proved himself fearless and asserted his authority over that pig and then given up the chase, arrived about the same time.

I was plastered up against the tree speechless and motionless. I could see and hear Daddy. I could see and hear Lincoln and I couldn't let them know. I was inside looking out. I thought I was going to be killed by a wild pig.

"Are you all right, Elizabeth Anne?" Daddy asked. I could hear him. I didn't know if I was all right. I couldn't come out. I felt as though I had pulled in so completely that I had become a pinpoint, a dot, somewhere in my body. It felt like it was right behind my eyes, the dot, that is – somewhere in my head. I wasn't afraid. I didn't feel afraid. I didn't feel anything. I was petrified. I couldn't move. I couldn't speak. I wasn't coming out and I was in a safe place that was a dot somewhere inside me looking out. I was stiff as a board. Daddy picked me up and went running down to camp with me. I could hear him yelling and screaming to Vance and Mother as he ran.

Vance and Mother came running.

"What's wrong?' Vance yelled.

"What's happened?" Mother screamed. "Is she hurt?" "Where?" And she started examining me as Daddy kept on running into the camp.

"I dunno," Daddy said. "She can't move and she can't talk," he said as he laid me on the table. Mother and Daddy and Vance all started feeling me all over to see if I was hurt. I knew they were doing it and I couldn't feel it.

"Oh, my heavens," Mother said. "What's wrong, Elizabeth Anne?" She sounded like she was really scared. I knew they were getting upset but I couldn't leave my dot even if I had wanted to and I wasn't sure I did. They all started squeezing and rubbing me all over. I knew it and I couldn't feel it.

"Does she have a pulse?" asked Daddy getting more frantic. Mother checked.

"Slow, but strong," she said.

"Then, she's still breathing?" asked Vance.

"I think so," said Daddy.

I wasn't moving. I wasn't talking. I was just in there. They didn't know what to do and I couldn't help them. I didn't know what to do. I was in there. I wanted to tell them I was all right but I couldn't. When Daddy checked to see if I were breathing. I didn't even know if I were breathing. I couldn't feel it. Gradually, their frantic turned to worry and concern.

"Should we take her into Happy Camp?" Vance asked.

"What good will that do?" Daddy shot back. "That nurse didn't know what was going on with Beck."

They all sat around the table with their hands on me. I wanted to come out. I just didn't know how. Mother had tears in her eyes. So did Daddy. I wanted to help them and I didn't know what to do to get out. Finally, I was able to move my little finger on my right hand. Mother saw it.

"She moved!" she yelled.

"Where?" screamed Daddy.

"Her finger. She moved her little finger." I was able to do it again so Daddy could see it.

In a little while, I could move my whole hand – then both hands. Gradually, my body would bend and they sat me up. They seemed to think if I could sit up, everything would be okay. I sat there for a long time. We all sat there for a long time. My dot was getting bigger and beginning to go through my body a little. Finally, I said, "I thought it was a wild pig."

Everyone laughed. I didn't mind their laughing. I think they were relieved.

"That was just a range hog, Elizabeth Anne. He wasn't coming at you. He was trying to get away from Lincoln. As soon as he saw you, he took off in the other direction. Range hogs are not wild boars."

Somehow, none of these explanations made any difference to me. The hog didn't matter anymore. What mattered was what had happened inside me. I had just experienced something they obviously couldn't understand or share and I didn't know what it was or how to talk about it. If I didn't, how could they? "I thought it was a wild pig," were the words that came out of my mouth but these were just words. What was important was what

I had experienced inside me – that I could go inside of me. That I had this pinpoint dot inside of me where I was completely safe, knew everything that was going on around me and didn't have to come out until I was ready. I was something separate from my body and could be in my body and no matter what happened to my body, I was safe. This was one of the most profound learnings and experiences of my life and it wasn't really about the hog. It was about me and I learned it as a five-year-old. Some people don't ever learn it, I reckon. I believe it took over an hour for me to come back completely.

This is Daddy's version – you can see that he just didn't get it.

> *One morning, I had to go up to the car for something. Old Lincoln was ahead of me. Elizabeth Anne was ahead of me, and all of a sudden I heard a pig squeal and here comes a pig down the pathway. There wasn't any way that pig could get off that pathway because Lincoln was chasing him down there. He was coming down there to get out of Lincoln's way and all of a sudden he stopped and saw Elizabeth Anne. She just froze solid, so I picked her up and took her back down to camp. Everybody worked with her and she finally decided she wasn't going to be eaten up by a little old pig. What triggered it off was that Vance and I had been talking the night before around the campfire about finding wild pig down in some hollow down in Arizona. We thought that would be a nice thing to do sometime. I don't know, I guess the discussion was about how mean they were . . . But anyway, after it was all over, it was kind of amusing to everybody except Elizabeth Anne. I think now she can look back and see it was somewhat of a laughing matter, maybe.*

Sometimes adults just really don't know what is going on. They just don't get or remember the important things. I let them think what they thought. It didn't really matter. I had my dot, my pinpoint inside.

## Picawish

I don't remember much about this and I do want to mention it as going was important to me. I don't know if I have the name right or if I am spelling it right. I am spelling it from what I remember phonetically. To my memory, Mother and Daddy never talked about it afterward and my father didn't mention it in his dictated memories of our time on the Klamath River. I do want to apologize for any five-year-old inaccuracies to the lovely native people of the Klamath River who had been like family to us during our stay. Here is what I remember:

We were invited to attend an important ceremony with the Indians there on the Klamath River. People who weren't members of the tribe usually didn't get to go or weren't invited. You had to be invited to go. I don't know but I think we had been invited because Mr. Beck was married to an Indian woman and one of our friends from Watts who lived there had married an Indian woman. And, we, ourselves, were Indians from Indian country in Oklahoma. So, in the way Indians are so open and everything – that made us family and we were invited to go to Picawish. All I know is that it is a very important ceremony that the Indians on the Klamath River have. Mother said that we were very honored to be invited. She told me how I should behave. I should stay close to her and Daddy and Mr. Beck. I should be very polite and treat everyone like an elder – which they would be. I should see how the Indian children were behaving and "act accordingly." I should be quiet and respectful because any ceremony like this was a special sacred thing. Mother said that this was their land, their home, and their ceremony and we were guests here. She said the best thing to do in a situation like that was to keep my mouth shut and my eyes open so I could see what was expected of me. She said she didn't know what was expected of her and that was what she was going to do.

I was so excited that we were going to Picawish. I didn't know what the word meant or what the Picawish ceremony was and it seemed like it was important here on the Klamath River, like going to Frenchy's magic place. It was something that "belonged here" and we were really lucky to have the chance to be a part of it and touch something most people would never have the opportunity to do. I knew it was a very spiritual thing that was close to the hearts of the people here that we had come to know and love. Mother said that we should always respect another's spirituality, that all spirituality was a pathway to the Creator and no one spirituality had all the answers. That was why we should respect all approaches as each had something to teach us. That sounded right to me.

When Picawish day arrived, I was almost as excited as I was about going to Indian Hop Mountain. The ceremony wasn't until night so I had to "keep myself busy" so I could "contain myself" until that evening.

Mr. Beck said that we should dress warmly and the women probably should wear long dresses or long skirts. Well, that was a problem for me. If I dressed warmly, I would wear long pants and a shirt and sweater and/or jacket. If I dressed politely, I would wear a dress with a jacket or sweater. I decided to wear my long pants with a dress over them and a sweater over that. I had asked Mr. Beck earlier that day what I should wear and he said since I was little, it was probably okay if I wanted to wear long slacks. I thought about it all day and decided that I wanted to be respectful <u>and</u> warm so I decided that I would wear my warm slacks under my dress and a sweater over my dress. Mr. Beck chuckled when he saw me and ruffled my hair (he did that sometimes) and said, "Good solution, Elizabeth Anne." (As an adult, this kind of solution, I call it the third option, has become important to me. When I become stuck in an either-or, I know to stop to look for the third option. It looks like I started this approach very early on in life.)

Picawish didn't start until evening, so just a little before dark Mr. Beck and all of us loaded in our car and headed to the ceremony. By the time we got there, it was getting dark. We parked the car and had to walk aways down toward the river. Mr. Beck did all right and we sorta helped him a bit on the steep places. By the time we got there, they had fires going. There were more local Indians than I had ever seen in one place. I had seen the local Indians when we went in town and such but they usually kept to themselves unless they knew you, so we saw quite a few familiar faces. There were lots of people here. Picawish was a big ceremony. I saw almost no white people. I suppose the few there had married Indian people and "belonged," and we seemed to be the only "guests." It was kind of a "private" ceremony. The fires were big and casting a glow and dancing light and shadows were everywhere. I didn't know much of what was going on and I knew just as soon as we got there that I liked it there. This was another magic Klamath River place. As soon as we walked into where the people were, the ones Mr. Beck and we knew rushed up to greet us. Then they started to introduce us to everyone at that ceremony. I believe everyone there came up to shake our hands, greet us, tease us, and talk a little. I felt like we belonged – like we were home. I don't know how to say it – it just felt like my insides were smiling. Mother said I could play with some of the other kids for a while. We just ran around mostly. She said when the ceremony started, I would have to be quiet. After a while, things quieted down and I went over and sat on Daddy's lap. Mother seemed so happy and peaceful. I knew she was enjoying herself like I was. It was like we were "back home" in Indian Country. I believe Mother and Daddy were sitting on a log. Mr. Beck told us that there would be some things that went first – I think like prayers and dances and things – I'm not really sure. Then, one of the young Indian men would "dance a canoe" across the river. We didn't know what that meant so he explained. The Indian man would be on the other side of the Klamath River and at a certain time, he would put one foot on each gunnel on either side of the canoe and, standing up, he would "dance" it across the river using no hands. I couldn't even imagine this. Was this the same Klamath River that had roared and churned under that strawberry-carrying thing that transported us over the river on the cable? Was this the same Klamath River that was so treacherous that cars went off in it and were never found? I couldn't believe it. I kept asking Mother and Daddy how he could do it. Was it really true? What if he didn't make it and drowned? Would they still have the ceremony? Wasn't he afraid? Didn't his mother and daddy worry about him? Would we be able to see him? I had a million questions and my answers were all, "Shhh, we don't know, Elizabeth Anne. Let's wait to see."

Mr. Beck and our other friends told us that there comes a point in the ceremony when all guests and outsiders have to leave. I got the impression that most of this whole thing was secret and it was really special that we had been invited as honored guests. Then there was a point when you had to leave or then you had to stay and participate in the whole thing and you couldn't leave after that point. When that time came and if you chose not to leave, you had to eat everything and do everything they did. Someone had hinted that they ate dog and I don't know if that was true. Mother and I wanted to stay. Daddy didn't. We were told that the time when we had to make the choice was when the young Indian man landed his canoe on the shore and the people moved into a new level of the ceremony. That would probably be sometime around midnight.

I must have dozed off because I remember the excitement around me when he pushed off from the other shore. It was already late then. I don't remember falling asleep. I just remember trying to keep awake.

The next thing I remember was Daddy shaking me gently and saying "Elizabeth Anne, wake up. It's time to go." Mr. Beck looked tired, too. Daddy carried me to the car.

Mostly the memories I have are feelings, not thoughts or visual. There were so many big people there that I couldn't see much of what was going on. Whenever I think of Picawish (and I have remembered the name of it for seventy-eight years. Can you imagine the impression it made on that five-year-old if I remembered the name so clearly at this point in my life?) I am astounded with how important the whole experience was to me. When I went back to visit the Klamath a few years ago, I went into the tribal offices in Happy Camp. The people working there were polite to me – and when I mentioned that I had attended a Picawish ceremony over seventy years ago, the chief came out and visited with me.) I felt happy, safe, warm inside, content and belonging. Whatever happened to me there was beyond thinking, beyond seeing. It took place deep inside my very spirit and remains there until this day. I belonged to a people.

## The Salmon Run

My father remembered it this way:

*By this time we started discussing just what we were going to do because there was no question but what we were going to get into war. In the mail, I got a notice from my place of employment that I should come back immediately and go to work. So, we decided that was what I would do, I'd just leave the mining equipment with Vance. Vance said he was just going to stay there and keep on mining. In about a week's time or so we would be moving. In that week's time the salmon started running.*

*We had become acquainted with a nice lady. Beck had married an Indian woman and she was some relation, I don't know how it worked out. Beck and his wife had two boys working for the forest service. But they were never available, always out of touch. I don't think we ever met them. Anyhow, they got word up to us that the salmon were running, so I take orders from Beck and Roscoe and John Thomas, and away we go down to the Falls which is a nice big falls on the Klamath River. This lady, being Indian or part Indian, I don't know which it was, had fishing rights. There is a big tribe down in there, I think the Hopa Tribe. She had fishing rights on the Klamath River for all time. We go down there, to catch the salmon, no luck. So, we unpack the mules and take off across the country with pack horses, we just take off across the country, God knows where they lived.*

*I think Roscoe's wife knew 'em. Well we'd met them a time or two. So we take off to go get some salmon for everybody. When we get out there, all the folks were talking. The lady tells her young son, "Take 'em down and show them where Dad's got his fish, and they can buy the fish."*

*Off we go down the hillside, down to the bank. The little boy shows us a pile of fish, and I asked him, "How much?"*

*He says, "Dollar apiece."*

*About this time his dad comes up.*

*"Those are not our fish, those are not our fish. Son, you know better than to tell him we'll sell somebody else's fish. We don't sell fish at all here. I never sell fish."*

*See the situation was that you are not allowed to make a commercial enterprise out of this fishing down there. We didn't know what to do. Here we had a kid telling us here's the fish for a dollar apiece and his dad comes up and says they are not his and he can't sell 'em. But about this time, Roscoe's wife come up and the other lady was with her. I guess she had heard what was going on coming down the trail.*

*"Oh, Dad, these people are all right," she said. And she told him who we were.*

*"Oh, yeah? Well you can have all you want," he said. So we started carrying fish out. We filled in the trunk in the back of a '36 Chevy. We filled that thing full of salmon. And the most amazing thing was well, this little boy was, I guess, about nine years old, and I think I have a picture of these fish. He just put those fish on the rope over his shoulder and the tail was dragging. He could carry quite a few fish and they were quite big. Anyhow, we get the fish and get them down to camp and divided them up between those who wanted them. I think Elizabeth Anne, you've got a picture of Roscoe's shack there, his home, must be, with ours and Roscoe's fish in front of it. Of course John took care of his and Beck took his.\**

*Anyway, we cleaned them and had them strung up. Manilla canned 26 quarts of salmon. Of course the rest of*

*them were mostly smoking them, but we were going to take
ours back with us. John took his over and he was smoking
them. I don't think Roscoe said much. But old Beck, he
hollered at John, "You're going to ruin those salmon."*

*"He's smoking 'em too fast," he said to us.*

*You know how a couple of old people get together, a
couple of old men anyway. One can't do anything right,
and the other one does everything wrong. Anyway, when
we got ready to leave we were pulling our stuff up on the
road, carrying it up there. The car came down Beck's road
with our load but when we were ready to go out we had
to carry everything up to the road. We had so much stuff
the car wouldn't pull it. It was about five o'clock in the
afternoon – here comes Beck, John and Roscoe down with
all these big salmon, all smoked, ready to go, and boy that
was really nice. They were rushing that salmon smoking
so we could take it with us.*

\* I still have the photos of those fish. That little boy
carrying the fish. And the fish laid out on the ground.
They were really something.

This is my version of the Salmon run:

We were slowly getting ready to leave the Klamath River. All of us
seemed sad and no one was happy to go. Daddy's job had called him back
and Mother and Daddy said we had to go. Daddy's work had said that he
was "essential to the war effort," whatever that meant. I think all of us
wanted to stay on the Klamath River. We loved it there.

Mother had been going through our stuff and giving a lot of it away.
We had brought things from the Ozarks like pecans, walnuts, canned
okra, squash, beans and corn. She said she figured that those folks in
California from the Ozarks would need it more than we did and Mr. Beck
and Frenchy – when they were picking those nuts out on a cold winter's
night sitting by the fire – why, they'd sure be thinking of us. I know that I
would be thinking of them. She also asked me to help pick out some of the
clothes I would outgrow soon and she picked out some of her and Daddy's
clothes that she said they probably wouldn't need. She gave them to Roscoe
and his wife and told them to give them to whomever needed them. I think
she thought Roscoe and his wife and his kids could use some and they'd
probably give the rest to the other Indians. She wanted to be careful not

to insult anybody. She even put in one of her good dresses that she had brought along that she thought would "fit Roscoe's wife and look good on her if she wanted it." When Daddy and Mother gave things to people, he said we needed to lighten our load. Besides, our gold mine had paid for everything and we were going home "with money to spare," Mother and Daddy said. I know they just wanted to give people things. They had all been so good to us. It's the way Indians do things.

Just as we were sorting through all our stuff and packing it up, Vance came running down the path and said, "The salmon are running." Mother and Daddy just stopped all that sorting and packing and said, "Oh boy, that's what we've been waiting for. It seemed like everyone just started running around camp doing something. Even old Lincoln was barking.

I asked "What are we doing?"

"We're going to go catch salmon," Daddy said excitedly. This sure sounded better than wild pig hunting!

I remember buying the salmon from the little boys. These salmon were so big. They were bigger than I was. I couldn't even lift one, and those little boys, who weren't much bigger than I was, carried several up from the river and up that steep bank. Some of them were so big that their tails dragged the ground when that boy threw them over his back. I was really impressed.

I asked Mother why that man had lied about their being his fish and Mother said, "Well, he wasn't exactly lying, Elizabeth Anne. He was just being cautious. He was afraid that we might be the law or the game warden or something."

"Why was he afraid of us?" I asked.

"Well, he was just afraid of a misunderstanding," Mother said. "It is always important to go by the law and we always try to do that. But laws are not made so that we would stop thinking for ourselves. Laws were made by people and sometimes people can make mistakes or just don't know enough.

"We always have the responsibility to think for ourselves and pray. Some of the laws weren't fair like those for colored people and Indians. Sometimes, when the law isn't fair, we have to abide by a higher law, God's law. We should be careful not to fool ourselves in situations like this," she said.

"Well, then why was he afraid we were the law?" I pressed.

"Well, the Indians are not supposed to sell fish. They can fish and catch it for themselves but they can't sell them. White men can sell them. The Indians can't." Mother said.

"That doesn't sound fair," I said.

"No, Elizabeth Anne, it isn't. You see," Mother continued. "That man didn't know who we were and he didn't want the law to think he was selling fish. When he found out that we were family because Mr. Beck had taken us in as family and Roscoe and his wife had taken us in as family, well then, it was okay for him to give us some fish and if we wanted to give him some money for those fish, well, that was okay, too. There's nothing commercial about that."

Mother said that the Creator has put something deep down in everybody that tells them right from wrong. They may try to ignore it but it's there. It's always there. We just have to listen to it. I was satisfied with that. It made sense to me.

# PART VI

# LEAVING THE KLAMATH RIVER AND THE TRIP BACK TO THE OZARKS

Mother and I spent a couple of days canning the salmon and then we headed out. We were going to go by way of Eureka and the ocean so we could see the ocean and the Redwoods once more before we headed back to the Ozarks.

### This is Daddy's memory of leaving –

*We didn't get very far down the road before it was time to stop and finally found a place wide enough. We were getting down toward the lower end of the river by then and finally found a place wide enough to pull off the road, throw the mattress on the ground and go to sleep. I had the mattress on the ground and about that time I heard some bones being crunched up in the brush. Couldn't see anything with the flashlight, and every time I'd turn a light up there, the crunching would stop. I'd turn the light away and it would go back to eating. Manilla had read about some fellow who went deer hunting up in the mountains and shot a deer. He carried half the deer down and went back after the other half and a mountain lion had found the deer and attacked him. That mountain lion clawed him pretty bad and they had to take him to the* hospital. So Manilla says, "Well, I'm not going to sleep here tonight with those bones crunching." I don't know what that is, so I said, "Okay," and the next thing I knew, everything was loaded on the trailer and she was back in the car. I didn't feel too good about sleeping there either, I must admit.

So we go on, way on. I guess we drove almost till daylight and finally stopped and slept a while. Then we went on down the road, went through the Redwoods and took a logging road and went down to some little town. I can't remember its name or what the road is. They had a big landslide. I see a little town there, and I think there was a grocery store or restaurant there. I'm not sure but I think it was Cove or something like that. There was a little river or creek came down to the ocean and there were a lot of fishing boats there. Of course the fishing industry has gone off the coast of California now.

Anyhow, we got to the ocean the next day quite early and old Lincoln, I couldn't figure out what he was barking at. The river where we stopped was up above the ocean quite a little bit. He was up on the bank and finally we figured out he was barking at the waves and everybody started laughing at him and kidding him and all. He went way down the road aways where he could bark in peace. And he'd bark every time a wave would come in.

We stayed there all the next day. We went out and got some shellfish and clams and put them in a fry and cooked them. They were not too good. We didn't know how to do it then. We didn't know you were supposed to drown them in seaweed first[32]. But they were pretty good and we went swimming and had a good time down there.

The next day we take off. We said, "Okay, that's the end of the trip, now we push for home," and we did. We drove till quite late at night and started early the next morning. About the second day out, the first day out from the ocean, we decided to sample that salmon. Well that smoked salmon had an awful lot of sampling because it didn't last too long. Boy, it was sure delicious. And from there on it was just a matter of sitting back behind the wheel and grinding the miles off as fast as I could.

---

[32] So they clean themselves before they are cooked.

(The trip back wasn't easy. Leaving the Klamath River wasn't easy. The incident with what Mother <u>thought</u> was the mountain lion was the source of as much teasing, laughing and hilarity as Daddy's forgetting the fishhooks was in years to come.)

Here's how I remembered the mountain lion incident:

I was sleeping in the backseat with Lincoln when we stopped at the wide spot for the night. Daddy unloaded the tarp and the mattress and threw them on the ground. While he did that, Mother made my bed in the backseat and settled me in. I could hear Mother say, "What's that Virgil?"

At first he said, "It's nothing, Manilla, go to sleep."

We were all pretty tired after packing and leaving and all. Then Daddy shined the light in the bushes. Then he turned it off. Then he shined the light in the bushes. Mother got up and said, "I'm not sleeping here."

"Oh, okay Manilla, I'll just go to the bathroom and get a drink of water, load up and we'll go on down the road."

While Daddy was puttering, Mother swung into action. She got Lincoln and me out of the backseat and poked us in the front seat. She single-handedly rolled up the mattress tight enough to get it stuffed in the back seat, folded that heavy tarp and tied it on the trailer, and plopped herself in the front seat with me on her lap, Lincoln in the seat beside her and the front and back doors on her side closed and locked. All this while Daddy was going to the bathroom and getting a drink. For years, Daddy wondered how she rolled that double mattress up small enough to stuff in the backseat by herself. Fear, I guess. She was not going to stay there a minute longer than she had to.

Speaking of fear, the Klamath River had one more go round of fear for me. Somewhere between Mr. Beck's and the ocean on the Klamath River Road as we were getting near to the ocean, there was a bridge that crossed the Klamath River. It was a steel bridge and the floor of it where the cars drove was like a grate. As you drove over it, you could look down and see the swirling, tossing water right under you. It was just like you could see the river where we were on that "thing" on the cable. I hated that bridge! And yet, I was fascinated by it at the same time. It was like the Klamath River was giving me one last chance to come to terms with it.

The trip home was hard, boring and tiring after we left the ocean and the Redwoods. We had left something behind that we would deal with forever and what we were taking inside us would change us forever. The Klamath River and those people were in us now.

# EPILOGUE

## Returning

We returned home to everyday life. I roamed the hills and fields as much as I could with Lincoln and our new dog, Shep. Then I started school. My father returned to his job as soon as we returned and Mother settled into running the house and whatever else she could get into. I remember the time she found a one-hundred-fifty-year-old recipe for plum pudding and decided to try it. It called for something like fifteen loaves of bread, so many pounds of suet, pounds of dried fruit of different kinds and a whole lot of stuff. Then, when she got it all mixed up, it puffed up – doubled or tripled in size and every pot, pan, dishpan, pressure-cooker or available bowl was utilized to contain the ever-expanding plum pudding. Everyone we knew received hand-decorated plum puddings for Christmas that year.

One of the most important realizations of our whole Klamath River adventure was that after the Klamath River, we "went our separate ways" so to speak. We moved back into a western culture way of doing life. No longer were the days spent with the four of us, Mother, Daddy, old Lincoln and me interacting all the time as we did our work, went off on our own, and came back together in the processes of our lives like the Indians of the Klamath River did. We were back in the white man's world. We were separated and segregated into age and sex groupings. Our work was separate from our lives. We adjusted and something vague, indescribable and very precious seemed to be missing. Life was more work. We didn't work harder. We probably worked less and life was more work. We still went on vacations. We still listened to stories. We still cooked together. And, the world seemed to pull us apart more and more. There was less flowing and more doing. Life's process seemed to become more and more segregated into isolated segments. We had been living like our ancestors on the Klamath River and that way of living was so easy, so integrated, so precious. Something, like an ancestral memory, had stirred within us that would slumber there for the rest of our lives. That "knowing" of a different way is still "alive and well" in me and, I believe, guides much of my life today. After Pearl Harbor, my father went to work for the Civilian Signal Corps, a work relationship with government agencies that would continue until his retirement. His brilliance in electronics asserted itself and he received some well-deserved recognition – not nearly as much as he deserved, I believed. He died in his late seventies, twenty-four years after my mother died. He had returned to visit the Klamath River several times before his death, taking the woman he married after my mother died at least once or twice. He seemed to need to return.

My mother survived my father's working for the government, moving around from place to place, and taking her away from her beloved Ozarks. She did this on the condition that she would be able to go back to the Ozarks every year to visit the graves of her ancestors and drink from Ballard Springs. She said she knew that if she returned and drank from Ballard Springs every year, she would always return. She did. She is buried there – a horsewoman until she died at fifty-three of injuries sustained when she was crushed against the barn wall while trying to train an unruly stallion. She was elected to the National Poetry Society before she died. The culture could never take her "Indianness" out of her and her annual trips to her roots sustained her no matter where we lived (She always maintained that New Jersey was the worst.)

And Lincoln, well, Lincoln got me through most of my formative years until I was almost ready to go to college. I guess he just stuck around until he decided I could make it on my own. He was my teacher, my parent, my guardian and my friend. We often talked about those days on the Klamath River like they were right then and there. He guarded each new car that came into the family and he never had to worry about being abandoned again for the rest of his life.

Marvin, the brother next to my father in age, was probably the unhealthiest of all the brothers physically and he lived the longest. He joined the Navy in World War II and became a cook, married and raised two sons. He opened his own butcher shop in Missouri in a town near his father's roots and cared for my grandparents in their old age.

Francis joined the army and was in the Battle of the Bulge. He was not physically wounded but his soul was. That happy, carefree, loving young man never came back. He became a veterinary assistant, married and raised a family but his heart and soul never returned. He died the first of "the boys" of a heart attack.

Leslie, oh, dear, sweet Leslie, my uncle/older brother. He was too young for the war, thank goodness. Sometimes, I think he was just too sweet and gentle for the world in which he found himself. He married a beautiful Cherokee woman and they worked in the Southeast for a while and raised a family, then returned to the Ozarks, to their roots where he died in his early fifties, leaving a wife and children who join me in still grieving him.

Grandma and Grandpa Willey continued the country store for many years. Some people never did pay them but Grandpa always said, "That's all right. They will when they can." When they retired, Grandma worked as hard as usual and Grandpa had time to listen to the radio and read a bit more. As they grew older, they sold the farm and moved up near St. Joseph, Missouri, which was where Grandpa had grown up. Grandma outlived Grandpa by several years.

Grandma Reed lived to be eighty-seven. I continued to spend part of my summer vacations with her until her death. She taught me about herbs and medicines, life and healing, love and dignity. She was always a lady and whatever I knew of being a lady I learned from her. She continues to be one of my greatest teachers.

My father has this to say about his last contacts with Vance.

> *I saw Vance back in the 1940's. I got in touch with him, I don't remember how I did that. Oh, yes I do. I went out to L.A. and took a special course in servicing precision radio instruments from a company that was making them. They wanted service people throughout the country and I felt this was a good side job for me. I think I spent two weeks of my vacation down in L.A. and I probably looked him up then, because I went out to see him. I think he was living in Pasadena. And a man of his intelligence, with the training I started him out in radio – he'd been doing service work there in L.A. During the army, he wound up as an officer candidate and was an officer in the Signal Corps – only to find that when I came back there he was winding some coils for the university there, and he was tied up in one of these pyramid schemes that always comes out of California, you know, where you start*

*up a little business and you have to buy your merchandise
from another guy who has a pyramid of the same group of
people and on up you know. And the products they were
selling were health foods – all grown on organic farming.
And they had a lot of pills to sell. One was alfalfa pills.
Now, there is nothing wrong with alfalfa pills. They have a
lot of good stuff in them. And there is nothing wrong with
vitamin pills. It was just the idea that it was a pyramid
scheme. I don't know whatever came of that. Of course
he came back from gold mining. He met this girl he had
been going with out there and they got married. She was
a beautician out there in L.A. working at some place and
I guess doing pretty good. It just surprised me that a man
of his intelligence was tangled up in that, and boy he was
tangled up in it, too. He went to a pep meeting while I was
there, and I don't know what all. We corresponded off
and on for maybe six months and I didn't hear from him
anymore, so I don't know what happened. So that is part
of the story of my friend Vance.*

I never saw Vance again.

I presume that Roscoe and John Thomas lived out their lives on the
Klamath River.

The Indians, though maybe not as visible (like the land) are still there.

My father went back to visit Mr. Beck several times before Mr. Beck
died. He said this about one trip there.

*He had a nice garden there. He showed us some grapes
and he had apple trees. Later on when we were out there,
he'd been trying to sell his fresh merchandise at either
Clear Creek or Happy Camp. The stores wouldn't buy it
because he didn't belong to a union, grower's union. If they
bought from him, the union wouldn't deliver to the stores.
Beck could sure have used the money. He had outstanding
grapes, squash, carrots and I don't know what all. In my
slides I have a color slide of him holding this stuff in his
hand. Of course he needed the money, he was on Social
Security. In those days, Social Security didn't pay much.
And today it pays less. I'm a little sour on this stuff, I know.*

*They just need somebody else and some responsible people in Congress. If we can get a good president, elect good senators and representation, they will handle the matters. President is just a figurehead – worthless anyway.*

Mr. Beck lived out his life in that big house he had built almost a century before. He lived to be well over one hundred. He was a good man and he was my friend. Whatever abuse he may have experienced as a boy, he never let it keep him from being a good person. He was part of the lifeblood of the Klamath River and when he died, his bones returned to the earth there. My father told me that Mr. Beck's house had burned down.

Frenchy, like all the others I have mentioned here, lives on in my memory and my stories. Mother was right! I still have his magical place on Indian Hop Mountain clearly in my memory and in my soul almost seventy-eight years later. In my mind, he was a brilliant, heroic man and lived the life of a hero.

Frenchy drowned swimming the Klamath River with a rope over his shoulder attached to a cable. He was trying to help someone run a cable across the river. I heard that after he drowned, some people took his cabin apart board by board because it was rumored that he had a fortune in gold hidden there somewhere. Fools! I'll wager that if he did have gold, it was in a bank or hidden in the ground somewhere. He was much too smart to hide it in his cabin. My father's last words about Frenchy were: "Frenchy's gold was in his mind." He really loved the wilds and that country. Our minds and memories are the best place to store our gold anyway.

The river took him. There is no known place where his bones are resting. His life is not marked by a tombstone <u>and</u> he lived an exotic and irrepressible life.

These are all noble people. They lived powerful and heroic lives. Their names may not be in the history books, yet, their lives were lived with meaning and purpose and they contributed to the majesty of the Ozarks and the Klamath River. Perhaps this book can be their tribute and Frenchy's marker.

Is there any such thing as an ordinary person? Clearly, there is no such thing as an ordinary life.

Me? I write books.

# Digging Deeper

I am an old woman now and age has a way of clearing our vision even as our sight dims.

As I finished this book, new awarenesses came flooding in about our time among our people on the Klamath River. I realized that two of the authors were very present in the voices in this book, my father and that five-year-old little girl. Yet, we had not heard much from the perspective of this eighty-two-year-old woman. Ah, she stuck her nose in once in awhile and, in general, she stood back and let them tell the stories as they remembered them, mostly without her interrupting or imposing her perspective. Then, as I sat with the manuscript, I realized that it felt incomplete and I finally knew what was missing was the perspective on these experiences that had evolved and played itself out in my life.

One of the most obvious awarenesses was that this time on the Klamath River had a surprising impact on all our lives. Relatively, in the scheme of things, it was a short time – only a few months. Emotionally, spiritually and developmentally, that time kept reverberating in all our lives – personally and collectively. There was something that had never and would not let us go. I think we all knew this fact personally and collectively and we never processed the impact nor attempted to put it into words. Maybe it was just too precious to tamper with. Yet, now, I feel I want to risk it.

I know after my mother died and my father retired, he returned to the Klamath River several times. He even drove his SUV and Airstream trailer down that road and described in detail how the road was still so narrow and the curves so sharp that he would have to "inch" the Airstream around a curve going forward, backing up inch-by-inch until both the car and trailer mastered the turn.

I know when he talked about the Klamath River, it seemed that he was almost seeking something lost or left behind and I was little help to him as I had my own fish to fry at that age. I think Mother might have been able to help him as she was the poet and had the bit of Irish that gave her the "gift for gab" but she was long gone and his new wife was patient, yet had no idea of the meaning or purpose of his search.

Now, after seventy-eight years, I think I may be able to add that perspective.

When we were there on the Klamath, we lived and functioned much like our ancestors lived. The secret he was searching for was not in the content of who, what, when's, it was in the process – the how, the unseen, the way – and he was too "scientific" to be able to grasp process. That was Mother's department. He truly believed in Western mechanical science and its ability to give us the answers we needed, even though his soul had other ideas.

On the Klamath, we lived in nature 24/7. We were nature. We felt and moved with the rhythms and processes of nature. We lived in process. Often, the weather dictated what we would do that day, regardless of what we had "planned" to do. Later in life, I found that living in Hawaii was very much similar to living on the Klamath for me. In Hawaii, I could say, "I'll get all my office work done today and then tomorrow I'll go to the beach." So, I would get my work done on that beautiful sunny day and the next day – it would rain. I soon learned why, when I first started living in Hawaii many years ago, on a sunny day many businesses would have signs on their doors that said, "Gone to the beach. Come back tomorrow." I soon learned everything got done – in process – in nature's time. It just didn't get done in the time and the way our minds planned it – as is the way with the living of life.

On the Klamath, we all worked hard and contributed whatever each of us had to contribute. We didn't have roles assigned. We just did what needed to be done. Clocks and watches were not needed, necessary or wanted. We knew where we were in time and space. There were no time-clocks or working hours. Yet, we all worked and gave what the moment demanded.

As I write this, I am reminded of what my dear friend Reuben Kelly, an Australian Aboriginal (he would rather be called Koori) gentleman once said to me. He said, "Before the white people came, we lived like English gentlemen. We didn't work for wages. We had everything we needed. It was like a Garden of Eden. Everything we needed was right around us. We had no medicines. We didn't need them. Our foods were our medicines. Our herbs and foods kept us healthy. We had lots of time for spiritual things like dancing, ceremonies and just being with and talking to the Creator. Ours was the good life."

Well, that "good life" is what I experienced on the Klamath River. Our foods, mostly grown and gathered right there were our medicines – especially when Mother and Frenchy seasoned them just right with herbs and spices. I don't remember any of us being sick during the entire time we were there. (This reminds me of visiting a German orphanage after World War II. Most of the children were "illegitimate" children of foreign – mostly American – soldiers. One of the facts we gleaned from that visit was that the kids who lived in tents – they were terribly overcrowded – were significantly healthier than those who lived in buildings!)

There was a daily flow of sharing – the land, the resources, time, stories, and whatever we had. There was no hierarchy. Those who had more gave more. Those who had less gave something else. We lived in harmony and balance. I don't remember being "punished" during that whole time nor do I remember any arguments between my parents or with anyone else. We truly lived in harmony and balance. No one took more than they needed and everyone put in what they could. We lived in balance with all around us. Life flowed. Life was easy. We worked hard and, indeed, the living was easy.

As I reflect back, what I see is that when we returned to Arkansas, our lives became busy. We were becoming "assimilated." We became devoured by a wage-earner society. We became enmeshed in an analytic, conceptual, reductionistic society. Daddy went off to work. I went off to school. Mother took courses at the university, took extension courses on food and these courses taught her that the healthy way to gather, prepare and serve food that she learned from her grandmother (my great-grandmother) and my father's mother were not "scientific" and therefore "not good." We all busily became focused on becoming part of and being successful in a technological, materialistic, mechanistic society. And, we did well. My mother had the most difficult time with this "assimilation" and insisted on a yearly visit back "to our roots, the graves of our ancestors and the Indian country of the Oklahoma Territory." Out of her "house money," she bought twenty acres there – ten of which were given to my uncle Leslie when he needed it and ten of which I still have.

"We shall always have a place to return to," my mother reminded us many times.

Writing this story has "returned" me in so many ways. It has returned me to the wisdom of Selu, the corn mother. I have her portrait, as interpreted by a Cherokee artist, hanging in the home I bought/built when I returned to the land of my ancestors over 15 years ago.

We are like Selu, the corn. We have all the wisdom, the depth of spirituality and the connection with all creation that we need to sustain us and our people buried deep inside of us where it has remained in spite of attempts of assimilation by ourselves upon ourselves, and by others. Our ancestors and the Creator have not abandoned us. They have only been waiting for us to remember and call upon them for help.

My experiences as a five-year-old on the Klamath River have been one of the pathways that led me back to reality – the reality and wisdom of a way of living the process of life that is whole and healing to all creation – myself included.

I am grateful. What else can I say? I am grateful. As our ancient stories tell us, like the corn, each of us has within us what is needed to feed a starving world.

This, I believe, was what my father was seeking in some way to articulate for himself and this is what I needed to articulate in writing this book.

We now desperately need the wisdom of our ancestors. I needed to articulate this knowing of this experience for all my family and there are other things I feel I need to articulate to bring this book to a proper closure.

## Lincoln

Besides guarding the car, it was Lincoln's job to guard me and he took this job very seriously. He never left my side unless I was with one of the adults. When I was safely in the company of a <u>responsible</u> adult, he was excused (like you are from the table) and then he could explore, sniff, and snoop around as much as he wanted.

He was always with me when I went up the trail to see Mr. Beck. I would never go up there alone – Lincoln was always with me. When we went inside, he waited on the porch. When we headed for the garden, he ran ahead and inspected every inch of that garden to make sure there were no snakes or anything that would hurt us. Then he would lay down in the shade and keep an eye on us while we worked. He seemed to know that guarding children and elders was a very special job and he took it very seriously. When we left to go see Mr. Beck, Mother would always say to Lincoln, "Now, Lincoln, you keep a good eye on Elizabeth Anne and Mr. Beck, you hear?" And he always did just that.

Now the key here is responsible adult. He would go snoop and sniff around if I were with a <u>responsible</u> adult. Now, it is not that Mr. Beck was not a responsible adult. He most certainly was. Look at all he had done supporting himself at sixteen years old, building the big old house and raising a family. He was clearly a responsible man.

The issue was that now he was an elder – really an elder at 92 and it was time for others to take care of him some of the time and Lincoln and I certainly did that. We were both honored to take care of Mr. Beck.

I never cease to marvel at how much my five-year-old Elizabeth Anne remembers. She was only just barely five-years-old. I do marvel at how she whispers to me and corrects me if I get something wrong. She is still polite and she still calls me "Miss Anne" as she was taught to do.

She was an extraordinary keen observer. Of course, she had been trained to be since birth. Daddy always said, "Watch carefully Elizabeth Anne and you will learn more than any words will ever teach you." I keep hearing that little girl saying to me, "Miss Anne, don't forget this. Miss Anne, don't forget that." I think she fears I don't have a good memory. Maybe I don't, but "we" do.

Lincoln died when I was in high school as a very old and beloved dog who had helped raise me, taken care of all of us, and taught us to be better humans. Sometimes, dogs just know more about being good than humans do. As I look back over eighty years, I can see that the four-leggeds in my life had great patience with me and shared their wisdom unselfishly – always.

## The Car

I am aware that our relationship with the car and the way we used the car was very different when we weren't on the Klamath.

On the Klamath, mostly, the car sat there for weeks and never moved except every two weeks or so – or when needed, we took it to town.

On the Klamath River, the car was never used to separate us, like it was when we went back to Arkansas. We just came together closer when we used the car – like the time we drove Mr. Beck that 90 miles with a ruptured appendix.

Normally – we walked when we went somewhere and everything was close.

Yet, when we returned to what was called "civilization," the car became the vehicle for separation – except on long trips which were usually vacations. The car took on the role of taking us away from our life and work together. It did not "bind" us as it did on the Klamath River.

On the Klamath River, we lived "vacation" even though we worked hard.

# Frenchy

As I think back, strangely enough, I can't remember what the outside of Frenchy's cabin looked like. I do, however, remember the inside clearly.

I remember that it was a ways from our camp and we usually drove there, parked the car on the side of the road and walked up the hill to the cabin. It was on the hill side of the road and going to Happy Camp. Mr. Beck's place was on the river side of the road.

I always remember how neat and clean and simple Frenchy's cabin was. There was nothing "extra" there. Everything was used and useful.

At first I had trouble understanding Frenchy. Everyone out there talked different from the way we talked except Vance, Roscoe and John Thomas, but I could understand them pretty well but not Frenchy. He was a different matter entirely. It didn't take us long though because he talked with his hands and his whole body and soon I understood Frenchy's "English" just like I understood Mr. Beck.

I decided right then and there that it was good to learn about people from everywhere, learn what they know and how they speak.

Mother and Daddy said that the world is a big place and we should know as much as we can about all our relatives.

I came back from our time on the Klamath River with all kinds of relations I never knew I had.

As I said earlier, Frenchy died in his beloved river doing something for someone else. That all seems so appropriate to me. That's how and who Frenchy was as I knew him. I didn't care what the French Foreign Legion thought about him. He was a good man. Mother, Daddy, Lincoln and I always knew that in the depth of our beings.

Frenchy was family and friend, and a teacher who opened our eyes to a much wider world. He had a quick brain and a heart full of love, which he shared freely with those who could accept it and we and the Indians of the Klamath sure knew how to accept that love – without judgment.

That was a good thing – for all of us.

In looking back, I see that Frenchy was my first glimpse to a wider world and an awareness of the goodness in everyone regardless of their past or what people say about them. He and my parents taught me that it is what is in a person's heart that counts in the end and, regardless of who you are, we are all family if we can just find the way back to that knowing.

We lived that knowing with the varied people on the Klamath. The river demanded it.

# Learning

There is always something to learn and at five, I was an empty vessel begging to be filled. Mother and Daddy took that need to learn very seriously. They were always saying, "Look here, Elizabeth Anne, see how this works? Can you see how it is made? Look here, can you see how the dung beetle walks differently from the praying mantis? It's good to know your bugs – some are very friendly to humans, some are not so much and some are downright dangerous – just like people. You have to learn to know which is which. Everything – every one is unique."

Years later, an Australian Elder told me – "Our old 'womens' started teaching our children when they were in their mother's womb and the minute they was born, they taught them. By the time they were five or so, they had the equivalent of a Ph.D.'s education."

That is what it seemed like to me – I was constantly being taught. My father wanted me to learn what he knew in the Indian world – hunting – shooting – fishing – survival.

And he wanted me to know as much as I could about the white world – math, science – He was always teaching me.

My mother made very sure I knew my <u>and others'</u> Indian world. She said this history and these people and their ways were being overrun and it was important to know as much as I could about it all – especially the history and the way of life. It was a good way of life.

And she also wanted me to learn about literature, poetry, and now I realize – psychology, so I could understand people. Understanding – was very important to my mother. She would always say to me, "Always remember not just to see what people do; try to understand <u>why</u> they do what they do. When you understand that, you will feel differently about them."

My great-grandmother seemed very concerned that I know how to heal, gather medicine, prepare medicine and in a healing way be able to be quiet and listen – to everything, even the rocks.

I was never not being educated. So often I heard – "We'll just have to forgive them. No one ever taught them the right way to live."

I was taught respect and honor in relation to everything – the people around me in Arkansas and Oklahoma knew that – the people on the Klamath River knew that. No one ever locked their houses or cars – even when they had their bags of gold dust in them – but things have changed on the Klamath River – and everywhere else.

I was so lucky to know that time and that river when I did.

I now know that there is embodied and disembodied learning. The embodied was more fun and more meaningful and the disembodied was okay too. Playing around with ideas – Yet, I was taught that it was very important to remember that concepts and ideas were not real. They are abstracts, approximations. That's the difference.

The Klamath instilled in me my knowing of this differentiation very early on.

## Spirituality

I have been taught that every group – every people – has been given a piece of the truth by the Creator. It is necessary that each group preserves their truth and passes it on and that we learn as much as we can about each group's truth so more pieces of the puzzle can come together.

Wherever we lived, Mother tried to learn the truths that each place and each people held dear.

I remember when we were in Utah for awhile and Mother studied Mormonism just like wherever we were she studied the local native beliefs.

"The Mormons are good people," she said. "They just have some differences."

Differences were always a gift to Mother.

We went to church in Oklahoma and one day I asked her why we didn't go to church in California on the Klamath River.

"We were already in church. All the time," she would respond

That seemed right to me.

I have always marveled at how a five-year-old girl could remember the name "Picawish" for so many years. It seemed that I needed to add my experience of this ceremony to the epilogue as it was probably the highlight of my time there.

So I called the tribal offices of the Karuk tribe there and was privileged to have a conversation with one of the young (in his 50's) spiritual leaders.

I had just seen a special segment on NBC Nightly News about the salmon returning to the Klamath and tears came to my eyes so I knew without a doubt that, as with all life in process, this book was being finished at just the right time – for myself – and maybe for some others too.

I asked if I had remembered the name correctly and was assured that I had. I asked for the correct spelling and, as I expected, was told that there was no real way to express it in English and that Pikyawish would probably be the closest expression of the word.

Then we chatted like long-lost friends.

I told him what I remembered and how I was more than impressed with the young Indian man "dancing" the dugout canoe across that treacherous river. He told me that is only possible in a very short window of minutes when the tilt of the earth in relation to the moon is at a certain stage and just the right angle. The young man, who has carefully prepared himself with proper face paint and prayers, has to be in such perfect attunement that he can use the gravitational pull of the universe to "dance" the canoe across. I knew what he was saying was true.

I asked if the ceremony was still "closed." He said that it was never closed to those who understood, were respectful, and attuned to the real meaning. Clearly, that was my family. Those who were not so attuned would be asked to leave.

He asked what I remembered most about Pikyawish. I became quiet and then said, "It was one of the most spiritual experiences I have ever known." We both were quiet together.

He then talked with me more about the meaning of the ceremony. That it is about renewal of the entire world and bringing all things back in balance. We both knew that we, as humans, have been out of balance and need to return.

He said that we can ask the Creator for help and that we have forgotten how to ask the Creator in the right way to get back in balance. We need to ask the best we know how and the Creator needs us to work hard and learn to ask the right way.

We then talked about the salmon ceremony and his training with an eighty-four-year-old elder to learn to prepare himself properly and learn the ceremonies. He has devoted himself to the learning for over 15 years. We understood one another and I knew that our work was coming together for a reason at this time.

It is time to return to the Klamath.

We talked about launching this book there at the time of the ceremonies.

The salmon are returning to the Klamath. This year was the best run for many years.

This is the time for world renewal.

# The Klamath River – Returning to Balance

Then there is the river herself . . .

No longer is she a roiling, boiling, swirling, twirling, tempestuous force of nature careening and thrusting her way to her home, the sea. No longer is she unmindful of anyone or anything that may venture into her way as she cuts through rocks and earth on her unheeding flight from the confines of the land – the eternal struggle to complete her cycle crushing cars, humans, granite in her endless quest for "home" understood only by the local Indians along her way.

On NBC Nightly News, when Brian Williams said that the salmon have returned to the Klamath, I heard a young Native man say, "We understand the salmon." Tears came to my eyes as they spoke of reclaiming the Klamath and possibly removing the dam. Maybe the time has come.

Yet, like us and the road, the Klamath River has become "tamed," assimilated into a technological, mechanistic, materialistic culture and "subdued." She has been dammed or damned to extinction – or has she?

Like old Mr. Beck and Frenchy, who were there to help us know and remember what it was like, we too must needs all we meet to remember, so we can rise above the focus on the material and pass on the essence of the unseen and the unknown that helps us remember all levels of reality.

Perhaps in letting that river into us, we let ourselves into us. Perhaps at this point in human history it is the returning that will teach us what we need to know.

I loved – and feared – and held that river in awe. I've heard people say that about God – somehow it seems different . . . and yet the same.

In the musical *Big River*, the only "love song" in the entire musical is a young man singing to his love, the river. That song always reminds me of how I felt/feel about the Klamath. She was so wild and beautiful and I have never stopped loving her.

I know the salmon meant something special to my mother.

We had never seen salmon before in Oklahoma/Arkansas in 1939.

Mother and our friends there on the Klamath smoked salmon.

She canned salmon.

And we had a little fresh fish to take with us on ice for the early part of the trip back.

She was bound and determined to take some of that salmon back to the Cherokee in Oklahoma so that our family and friends there could see and taste and ingest (know) what our California family had as gifts from the Creator.

We came to find gold, and, indeed, we found enough to support us and pay for that entire trip with a little left over to help us "start up again" back home with our people.

And, as Mother said, what we brought back from the Klamath River was much more precious than gold. We have memories, we have connections, we have family and we have an awareness that family is everywhere – which has been borne out again and again throughout my life.

Each of us has a role to play and if we do it, the far-flung pieces of the universe can come back together and function as a whole.

And, as it is with the river – it is with us and vice-versa. One cannot heal without the other.

This book is my love song to the river and the renewal of the universe.

I was walking by a stream today and was rushing to get someplace when I realized the need to slow down and heard the stream talking to me. It talked of process and living our process as it lives its process. To do that, it too has to "die" as it changes form from flowing water to vapor to cloud to rain to flowing water to the sea. It never complains. It has no fear of the change in its material form. It does not fear death or complain about this form-change. It flows and participates in its process.

The water can teach us so much about our lives – and does if we listen.

I was taught that we Cherokees are responsible for four things:

- To honor the Creator which is our primary relationship –
- To honor all creation –
- To be of service –
- And to preserve and practice the ceremonies.

I believe my Karuk family shares the same wisdom and responsibilities in their own way.

It's easy to live this way . . . if you just don't think too much.

Printed in the USA
CPSIA information can be obtained
at www.ICGtesting.com
LVHW041912091123
763554LV00005B/61

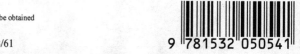